A Magical Journey

Your Diary of Inspiration, Adventure and Transformation

By

_____

A MAGICAL JOURNEY: Your Diary of Inspiration, Adventure and Transformation

First edition US copyright © 2010 Serene Conneeley

All rights reserved. No part of this publication may be reproduced, stored in a retrieval system or transmitted in any form or by any means, electronic, mechanical, photocopying, recording or otherwise, without the prior written permission of the publisher.

Conneeley, Serene
A Magical Journey: Your Diary of Inspiration, Adventure and Transformation
1st US edition
ISBN: 978-0-9805487-1-6
    203.5

Published by Blessed Bee
PO Box 449, Newtown, NSW 2042 Australia
Web: www.SereneConneeley.com
Email: SevenSacredSites@yahoo.com.au

Cover: Daniella Spinetti
Cover photo: Serene Conneeley
Illustrations: Justin Sayers

Love and gratitude to my sweet husband and precious beloved Justin, for making me endless cups of tea as I worked, motivating me when I was too tired to keep going, drawing all the beautiful illustrations, inspiring and encouraging me to follow my heart, and seeing my potential and my light even when I couldn't... Love and faery hugs to lovely Lucy, for the magic we continue to weave together... And love and deepest thanks to gorgeous Daniella, for her wonderful artwork, sweet nature, kind heart and immense generosity of spirit...

"I never travel without my diary. One should always have something sensational to read on the train."

Oscar Wilde, 19th century Irish playwright, poet and author

"An unexamined life is not worth living."

Socrates, fifth century BCE Greek philosopher

About the Author

Serene Conneeley is an Australian writer with a fascination for history, travel, ritual and the myth and magic of ancient places and cultures. She's written for magazines about travel, spirituality, health, news, environmental and social issues and entertainment, and contributed to books on witchcraft, psychic development, personal transformation and history. She is a reconnective healing practitioner and has studied magical and medicinal herbalism, angel therapy, reiki, shamanism and other healing modalities, as well as politics and journalism. She is the author of *Seven Sacred Sites: Magical Journeys That Will Change Your Life* and the CD *Sacred Journey: A Meditation to Connect You to the Magic of the Earth*, and co-author, with Lucy Cavendish, of *The Book of Faery Magic* and *The Book of Mermaid Magic*.

www.SereneConneeley.com

Praise for Seven Sacred Sites

"This is by far the best travel book I've read this year. Serene Conneeley's style evokes the great travel writers like James A Michener, who weave cultural anthropology seamlessly into an entertaining traveller's tale; a recipe for pure reading pleasure. I'd recommend it to any armchair traveller – and it's absolute gold for those interested in the spiritual traditions that continue to shape our world." *Joanne Lock, travel editor, Spheres magazine*

"This is a book that is a sacred journey in itself. Walk through its pages, and you may be drawn to one of the magical places on your life path. But the spirit of them lives within the book, so they speak to you as you travel in your mind inspired by the words." *Cassandra Eason, British author*

"Sometimes, if you're lucky enough, you will come across a book that has an energy so great it moves beyond its pages. *Seven Sacred Sites* is such a book. Brilliantly written and stunningly produced, the magical journeys within it will inspire you to dream, to travel and to ponder your own place here on our wonderful planet." *Kylie Matthews, Manly Daily reviewer*

Praise for The Book of Faery Magic

"This is a delightful guide that blends traditional faery lore with modern magical practices like guided meditation, setting up a faery altar and creating a wand, planting a faery garden and recipes and craft projects to deepen your relationship with the fae and discover your own inner wild self (not to mention have fun along the way!). There is a vast amount of information and a strong environmental message." *Bryony, Fae Nation*

"This is the ultimate guide to all things faery, and is entertaining, informative and enthralling. If you believe in faeries or are just curious, there is much to learn in this book, from history and legends, magical gifts and sites, to unique beings from around the world." *Larissa Chapman, Good Reads*

Contents

The Power of Journalling
The physical and emotional benefits of expressing your deepest self, exercises to awaken your inner voice and inspiration to begin your magical journey   2

The Wheel of the Year
Create magic in your life by attuning yourself to the sacred energy of the seasons and honouring these ancient festivals of the earth   20

The Cycles of the Moon
Make all your dreams come true by harnessing the power and magic of the moon as it waxes and wanes through its enchanted phases   54

Festivals of the World
Celebrate some of the beautiful spiritual holidays, rituals and events from around the globe   60

An 11-year Calendar
Keep track of the days, months and years, and co-ordinate your sacred celebrations with this yearly planner   96

The Book of your Life
Write the story of your life in the pages of this book, being inspired by the beautiful quotes that will motivate you to follow your heart and make your dreams come true   99

Expressing your deepest self

"Journal writing is a voyage to the interior."
Christina Baldwin, American author and spiritual teacher

A diary is a sacred, secret place to unravel and reveal your whole self. Whether you're travelling overseas or setting out on a journey within to discover your own truths, keeping a journal is a powerful way to make sense of the world, and of your own inner universe. Recording your experiences, emotions and insights leads to an understanding of yourself and your motivations, identifies what makes you happy and the things that drain you of energy, and illuminates the areas you want to focus time and energy on. It allows you to explore your psyche, and is a valuable tool of self-expression, self-discovery and self-knowledge.

Expressing the feelings at the core of your being can heal your heart and help you let go of past pain, forgive yourself and others for inflicting hurt, and move forward with joy and confidence. It reminds you of your inner strength and courage, provides clarity and context, and encourages you to consider your actions and beliefs, rediscover what you already know, re-evaluate your life and find a harmonious way to deal with the issues you face. Your journal is a mirror that reveals your shadows and light, showing you who you truly are and how to work towards becoming what you want to be.

Transforming into an observer of your life – not just of the events but also of your self and your emotions – can change your future. The act of observation is so powerful that it affects the behaviour of electrons in the field of physics. Equally, observing your own life can fundamentally change it by providing greater insight into how and why you do things and giving you a deeper appreciation of the inner workings of your mind. This creates a self-awareness that influences your reactions and leads to better choices, thus changing the outcomes and consequences. Being self-aware means you'll live your life more consciously and in the moment, which creates greater happiness.

Observing and writing about your life also adds deeper significance to every experience, because you pay more attention, feeling the emotions fully and remembering an event more vividly in order to record it. Re-reading an entry later can also add further weight, reminding you of what happened and allowing you to see it from a new perspective. Something not particularly memorable at the time can grow in importance later, when placed in context with other events or with the benefit of hindsight, because sometimes the full meaning is only revealed with time. In contemplating your actions and emotions in your journal, both as you write about them when they happen and in the future when you re-read your entries, you're able to see the threads that run through your life and the way they interconnect.

Conversely, things that seemed incredibly traumatic or heavy with emotion can sometimes become lighter with distance. Time does heal, and it also helps you see things from a new angle and in a new light. Something that was unbearable or confusing at the time might now make sense, lose its seriousness and impact, or be revealed as a valuable lesson that helped you get to where you are now.

Writing about experiences makes them seem more real and concrete, because it's so easy to forget, as time passes, the subtle emotional glimmer you felt while you were going through it. Much like a photo or even a scent can hurtle you right back to a specific moment, re-reading a diary entry can remind you of not just what happened but also how you felt, and overwhelm you with the intricacies and sensations of the time. When you recall an event from the past, it's easy to forget how brightly you shone and your impact and triumphs, and to start doubting that something could have gone that well – so you play down the good things and exaggerate the negative. Capturing your joys and achievements as they happen immortalises them forever, so you can recall all of the magic and enchantment in the future.

"Writing and expressing can heal us. It can focus, support and enhance our lives and wellbeing. Whether we laugh or we cry, whether through sorrow or joy, we can understand more about ourselves, and each other, through keeping a journal."
              Doreene Clement, American author

One of the most valuable aspects of journalling is that it helps you remember the lessons you've learned and stop making the same mistakes. Patterns of behaviour are often repeated indefinitely – who hasn't complained that they always attract the same type of person, or end up being treated the same way by the same lousy boss no matter what the job – but when you're in the situation you don't realise you've played it out before because the emotions always feel fresh.

But keeping track of the situations and people you seem to attract, and your actions and reactions to them, can reveal patterns, help you realise more quickly when you are repeating one, show you the reasons you keep manifesting the same lessons in your life, and highlight anything you can do to change the outcomes. If your relationships all end the same way, chances are that there's something you're doing that needs to be understood and reassessed, even if it's just the kind of person you're attracted to. It's not about assigning blame or fault, but simply noticing and being aware of the rhythm of your actions in order to prevent problems from occurring in the first place.

Seeing things written in black and white and noticing your patterns is a powerful tool of self-development and growth. Years ago I broke off an engagement after reading my diary, because I suddenly saw that I was, yet again, living out the same pattern I'd sworn I'd never repeat. As I read entry after angry, frustrated, tear-stained entry, I realised I'd been trying to tell myself for a while that the relationship wasn't bringing out the best in either of us. I'd been ignoring the signs, trying to be a good partner and blaming myself when things were difficult, but within the pages of my journal I'd been documenting my deeper truths.

Reading over all the pain and doubt I'd written about was a shock, and I was embarrassed that I'd stayed in the relationship as long as I had. If a friend had told me all the stories I was reading – the things I'd put up with, the compromises I'd made, the "I can't go through this again"s I'd ignored – I would have told her to leave in a heartbeat. Yet I'd been telling myself these things in my journal but not listening. Seeing the ways I'd diminished myself and the behaviour I'd endured and allowed written down in the pages of my diary made it so much more real to me. It was a wake-up call I couldn't ignore.

I'm so grateful that I kept a journal, and was able to explore my own heart, realise what I do – and don't – want, and avoid a mistake that would have made us both miserable. When I met my now-husband, who's also kept a journal for years to remind him not to compromise his self, we were both very conscious of our relationship patterns and past hurts, and able to deal with them in a loving way, nurturing each other and ourselves rather than getting defensive and lashing out.

It's also amazing what you can forget or overlook when you want to, or be convinced didn't happen that way, and keeping a journal can help you remember what you've been through and don't want to experience again. It's important to bear witness to your life and not let someone else – or yourself – get away with treating you badly.

A friend used to send me diary entries via email and ask me to remind her of all the awful things her on-off boyfriend did, as she knew she would forget, and he would talk her round, if it wasn't recorded somewhere. She was too scared that he'd find it to keep a diary herself, so I became that for her, a witness, a reminder, a mirror. This is the value of a journal – it reminds you of yourself if you forget.

Writing also makes you more aware of other people and their feelings through the perspective you gain by reviewing events, which increases your empathy and can improve relationships with friends, loved ones and colleagues. If you're upset with someone, journalling about the situation can uncover what it's really about for you, and help you work out how best to address it. Considering the situation from their perspective, and trying to understand their motivation and point of view, will also provide insight into the way they see things, improving your ability to communicate and helping resolve the issue.

> **"When individuals write about emotional experiences, significant physical and mental health improvements follow."**
> *Dr James W Pennebaker, American psychologist*

The process of writing about your life doesn't just improve your relationships, help you avoid mistakes, soothe your soul and enhance emotional wellbeing. Research has found it also has immense physical benefits. Journalling has been credited with increasing immune function and overall health, improving hormonal activity and other markers of disease, reducing symptoms in patients with chronic illnesses, lowering stress, halving visits to the doctor, bolstering your ability to deal with trauma and past emotional experiences, decreasing heart rate and anxiety, and boosting attention span and memory.

Dr James W Pennebaker, a psychology professor who's published several books about the power of expressive writing, believes journalling about traumatic situations, even for just 15 minutes a day, helps you come to terms with them quicker, which reduces their impact on your physical health. He's researched the effects of journal therapy for decades, and explains that creating a diary entry about a painful event is like completing a job, allowing you to essentially forget what happened. This occurs because once you take your most pressing memories and put them into story format, the mind doesn't have to work as hard to bring meaning to them. Writing helps create a coherent, reasoned story, leading to new meaning and understanding of the situation, and helping the brain digest the information and store it more easily.

Psychology professor Dr Kitty Klein also found that journalling improves physical health, from arthritis to asthma, as well as mental health and cognitive abilities. It increases concentration and memory function and decreases susceptibility to distraction, which translates into real life outcomes like better university grades and job performance. And even a century ago, influential Swiss psychologist Carl Jung encouraged his patients to keep a diary as a therapeutic tool, emphasising the value of understanding the psyche through self-exploration.

Journalling helps you cope with traumatic events by providing a way to work through the pain. Writing about what happened, and your feelings and emotions related to it, can help you understand it, put it in perspective and find some closure, which gives you a sense of control over the situation. Says Dr Klein: "We do not forget traumatic experiences, but expressive writing can transform our memories so we are not continually upset by unwanted thoughts about the events."

Writing your feelings down also decreases the power they have over you, because giving them physical form dilutes their potency and provides some separation from the painful experience, which helps ease stress, anxiety and depression. It's incredibly cathartic, releasing the intensity of your emotions and bringing order to the chaos. Writing about any hard times and darkness you've been through, and purging your heart of sadness, provides distance and perspective, allowing you to read about it as though from a third-person perspective, more dispassionately than when you're caught up in the feelings of it.

This is why writing a letter to someone who's wronged you can lift such a weight from your shoulders, even if it's just in your journal and you never send it. Not only does it bring clarity and validate your perspective, but it also provides an outlet for your angst and tempers the intensity of your feelings, releasing your attachment to the trauma. You won't stop thinking about the hurt altogether, but it will lessen the power it has over you and its effect on your life and behaviour.

Writing to the person, even though they'll never see it, can help you come to terms with the issue without having to confront them, and neutralises their impact on you without them even being aware of it. It's astounding how quickly this process can provide you with a sense of relief and peace, and how dramatically it can change your outlook. Resolving it in your own heart allows you to let go of the energetic connection you have to a person or event, regardless of their attitude and whether or not they change their behaviour. It's a personal form of healing, and they don't even have to know you've done anything.

Journalling also brings clarity as it creates structure to the whirlwind of your mind. If you feel overwhelmed by your emotions, confused about how you feel or unsure of what you want to do about something, jotting down the issue, your thoughts and the possibilities available can help you get in touch with your inner self and access your subconscious, allowing new ideas and a sense of flow to emerge.

Writing a problem down can remove the mental blocks around it, letting emotions and truths spill out in a way speech or thought doesn't. It also sparks your mind into finding a solution by connecting to the creative part of your brain and letting the answer surface. You usually already know the answer, you just need to become aware of it. As you write you'll reveal things to yourself from deep within, and like word association, one sentence will inspire another, and you'll often find you've written down the way forward without being consciously aware of it. This leaves you calmer, especially if you end a session with a resolution to, or some insight into, something that was bothering you.

"It's really fun to read your journal a year later and realise how much you've changed. You look at something you said, something you really meant at the time, and it's like: 'I can't believe I ever really believed that!' That's the greatest thing about growing up."
Cameron Diaz, American actress

Journalling can also help you manifest your dreams, because putting your thoughts on paper and expressing your intent is the first step to making your goal a reality. Writing about a desired outcome takes the energy of the idea out of the etheric and into the physical and makes it far more real. Outlining the result you're aiming for helps you focus on how to make it happen, and illuminates the path you'll need to take to get there. It brings clarity to your planning and reminds you of the goal and the actions required to reach it. And once you start tracking your progress and recording all the little successes you have along the way, it boosts your optimism, increases your motivation and keeps you on target to achieve your dream.

When I was writing my first book I had a goddess calendar on my wall that I used as a progress journal. Every day I would make a note of what I'd done towards reaching my goal, be it completing another thousand words, researching a topic, getting the photos I would use reprinted, interviewing someone or calling an artist. Writing down all my actions and little achievements made me realise how much I was actually doing, which was especially helpful when I had writer's block or felt like I'd never finish. It also motivated me to keep going, because not only did I love being able to add something to the wall each day, but it made me realise how much progress I was making, and this filled me with anticipation and excitement and inspired me to continue.

Keeping a journal can also help you identify what your dream is and work out how important it is to you. By exploring your inner world, you'll discover where your heart lies, and what you're really passionate about. If you're always saying you want to do something – hold an art exhibition, change jobs, travel the world, be a yoga teacher – but you keep putting it off or making excuses, you might need to reassess. Perhaps it was a childhood dream that has been outgrown, a parent's plan for you, or something you like doing as a hobby but not enough to commit the time and energy necessary to take it to the next level. Lots of people say they want to do things – write a book, be an artist, work for a charity – but when it comes to the crunch they just don't want it badly enough. If you really want to make your dream come true, you would have made a start by now... or be about to!

It's okay to change your mind, or be so happy living your life that you don't need to pursue anything extra, but if you want to discover what makes your heart sing, reading over your journal will provide clues. Try to get in touch with the deeper dream, the one thing that will truly bring you to life, because once you know what it is, you'll do anything to achieve it. Writing about the reasons you feel you haven't reached a goal yet, and the obstacles you think are holding you back, may reveal what it is that fills you with passion and fire, and ignite an overwhelming urge to make it happen. Periodically updating your list of what you want to do, why you want to make it happen and how life will change if you reach your goal will also offer insights to your greater purpose and the pursuits that will provide meaning for you.

Tips for going within

"Journal writing is crucial to recognising those parts of ourselves we have shunned. It's like a mirror. When we first look into it, the blank pages stare back with ominous emptiness. But if we keep looking, we begin to see the face that's looking back at us."
Marion Woodman, Canadian psychoanalyst and author

- Start writing whenever the mood takes you. While it might suit your sense of neatness and order to begin your journal on January 1st, your birthday or the first day of a new job or overseas trip, you don't have to wait until then. Any day is a good day to begin.

- Write freely. Don't edit yourself, correct spelling, worry about grammar or rip out pages and start again – simply let the words, and the emotions, flow out on to the page. It's more important to get your feelings down. Later you can re-read it to find the pearls of wisdom, but when you're in the moment just write whatever comes to mind.

- Don't give up just because you miss a few days. Sometimes the lack of an entry can say just as much as a written one. Start again as soon as you can, but don't stress about catching up on what you missed at the expense of the colour and tangible emotion of the present – trying too hard to fill in the blanks can keep you permanently behind.

- Describe your mood at the beginning of a journalling session, then again when you've finished. It's amazing how quickly your state of mind can change, and often simply writing about an event or a depressed mood will help you work through it and lift the sadness, and you'll feel calmer and happier. If you see a pattern in what it is that helps soothe your soul, be it writing, questioning yourself, calling a friend or going to the gym, remember it for next time.

- Follow your inspiration. Some days drawing a picture, sketching some symbols, writing a poem or copying down an inspiring quote or lyric may be the best way for you to express yourself. There are no rules, so just follow your heart and your emotions.

- Take note of when you write. Do you only open your journal when you're depressed or you've had a fight with your partner? If this is the case, make an effort to write when you're happy too, or when your partner has done something romantic or you've had a great day, even if it's just a few words. It will help you see your life in a more positive light, and reinforce the good times. If you focus too much on the negative you can overlook the good, and likewise the reverse.

༄ Record the time you write too, because your state of mind might be quite different depending on whether it's morning or night. Perhaps there's a time of day that you're more reflective, and more likely to open up and have realisations about your life and your self. Also write down where you are – snuggled up on the couch with a cup of tea, snatching a few minutes between meetings, on the train to work – as your surroundings can also influence the tone of your journal.

༄ Write down not just what happened, but how you feel about it. Insights usually come after you've outlined the event itself and started to tap in to your visceral response to it. Allow the description of the experience to spark your deeper emotions and responses, and try to express everything you're feeling, good and bad.

༄ Try to journal even when you don't think you have anything to say, because the very act of writing opens up your mind and allows your thoughts to flow outwards. Often once you start jotting things down, one thing will lead to another and you will think of things to add.

༄ If you're really upset, the first page or two might be an almost unintelligible outpouring of pure anger or sadness. But if you keep writing, you can get beyond the raw emotion to the truth of the matter, and understand yourself – and others – better. Often answers are revealed when the process of writing connects your brain and your heart and lets what's buried in your subconscious emerge.

༄ Experts suggest writing for 20 minutes a day or more, several times a week. If you're really busy, at least scribble down a few quick observations or notes, a few sentences that reflect how you feel that day, or a few words regarding your emotional state. It will add to the rich tapestry of your longer entries, will jog your memory when you re-read it later and may help reveal a pattern to you.

Shifting writer's block

Sometimes you might want to write, but feel stuck about what to say or where to begin. Here are a few exercises you can explore to see what comes up. They'll help you delve into your psyche and trigger personal realisations to get you back into your journalling.

༄ Have a free writing session to uncover your inner thoughts. Set a timer for 10 minutes and start writing, as fast as you can, until it goes off. Write whatever comes into your head, regardless of how silly it sounds. Don't even think about what it means, just write. The mind is never empty – it can't help but think of things – so scribble them down. When your time is up read over what you have, and if there's a topic you want to explore further, begin again, focusing on that.

❧ Write down what you want to achieve by this time next year, and start exploring how to make it happen. What's the first step you need to take? What can you do towards it today? Next week? What's stopping you from starting right now? Commit to doing something small towards your goal every day, and record your progress in your journal.

❧ Consider your spiritual views. What do you believe, and why? Most beliefs, morals and perceptions are picked up subconsciously – first from parents, then from teachers, friends or partners – and often we don't even wonder whether they're right, or fit our adult life and the experiences we've had. Understanding why you think or act the way you do, and whether a belief still fits with the person you've become or should be discarded, is a good angle of self-reflection and development.

❧ Ponder what you most want to change about your life, and explore what's holding you back from doing it already. What would help you achieve it? How would your life be different if you did this thing? Do you actually want it to be different or are you happy as you are? If there's a character trait you want to develop, write about why. What would you need to change about yourself to display it? How would you change if you adopted this characteristic? Start practising it now.

❧ Write about who inspires you the most. It could be a friend, a co-worker, a humanitarian, an actor, a politician or a fictional character. Describe what it is about them that you admire so much, then explore how you can be more like them in outlook. Write about a current personal situation from their perspective, outlining how they would handle it. Try to work out what your admiration for them says about you, and what you can learn from them and apply to your own life.

❧ Think about what it is that defines you to other people, be it your job, your vegetarianism, your spirituality, your tattoos or your purpose. In your eyes, how important a part of you is this? Do you feel you've outgrown this perception? Do different friends see you in different ways? Write down how your best buddy would introduce you to someone, and how you'd describe yourself to a stranger. How similar are they? Which one is the "real" you, or do you have many sides?

❧ If there's something you're avoiding doing, explore the reasons why. Do you really want to do it, have to do it or just feel that you should? What would happen if you didn't? I beat myself up for ages because I kept trying to learn Spanish, signing up for classes and being really diligent, then giving up and starting again a year or two later. It was an immense relief to finally realise that it's not because I'm lazy, I simply have other priorities. (I studied herbalism without any trouble, wrote a book and went to yoga instead.) If you really want to do something you probably will, so if you're putting something off, examine your motives. Letting go of the things you're not really passionate about will free you up to pursue what you do want to do.

☙ In the spirit of self-awareness not judgement, think about your worst "fault". Do you try too hard to please people? Are you particularly pessimistic? Do you care too much – or too little – what people think of you? Explore whether this is a childhood pattern or a defensive mechanism designed to protect you, and how it might serve you. Some supposed flaws have a purpose, protecting you from disappointment or pain, and others are outweighed by their positive aspect. But if it's affecting you in a negative way, consider how you can let it go.

☙ Another way to connect with your inner truth is to sit quietly and jot down a question about a situation you're facing with the hand you write with, then start answering it with your other hand. When you can finally decipher the scrawl, you'll discover some incredible pieces of wisdom, which were within you all along. Using your non-dominant hand connects with a different part of the brain and accesses the subconscious, so you'll learn a lot about why you act the way you do. It's all about unlocking the energy, power and knowledge you already possess, and going deep within to learn what you already know.

Different kinds of journals

"Journal writing is a way of paying close attention to our lives. A journal provides a gentle setting in which healing can occur. It offers one place where literally and symbolically, all of the pieces of one's life finally come together."
Marlene A. Schiwy, American author

Within the pages of this book you can write the story of your own life, mapping the highs and lows and triumphs and tragedies in whichever form suits you best. It doesn't matter how you journal, just that you start observing and recording your life in some way, looking within and learning about your own beautiful self. Here are a few ideas that might inspire you to begin exploring your inner world.

Travel Journal

When I started this project I was planning for it to be a travel diary and companion to *Seven Sacred Sites*, with maps, conversion charts, lists of international dialling codes and time differences, tips and travel advice, but the more I wrote and researched, the broader its scope became. Yet a big overseas trip can be the perfect time to start a journal, or begin another one, because you're guaranteed to have lots to write about, with new sights, new sounds, new people, new cultures and new ways of thinking opening up before you. Being away from home also gives you more time to write, because you have fewer commitments and so much more freedom – not that you should spend so much time recording your adventures that you stop having them!

My travel journals usually end up being half about the places I'm visiting and half about my inner journey, because new experiences trigger new emotions and challenge your viewpoint and beliefs, which is always a good thing. It also makes you think hard about yourself in terms of what is important to you, what you miss about your normal life, and the things that mean the most to you. Far from home and the everyday grind of work and routine, you are provided with an unusual perspective on your life, and will see past events, relationships and emotions with a distance that offers immense insight.

Today most information is easily accessible online, so printing up pages of international dialling codes and translating "hello" into fifty languages seemed a little unnecessary, but you may want to list your itinerary in the back of this book with your flight times, accommodation details, time differences for the places you're going to (check out www.timeanddate.com/worldclock or the World Time section of www.whitepages.com.au, where you can print out a chart comparing the time in your hometown to the time at your destination), area codes you'll need, your passport number, insurance details, conversion rates (they change often, but you can get a good idea at www.xe.com) and medical information such as your blood type, allergies and any vaccinations you had to have. You can also rule up a page with a few columns to keep track of your expenses or write in the names and contact details of new friends you meet along the way.

Blessings Book

Living with an attitude of gratitude can lift depression and transform your life. And it's not that hard to start seeing the world in a new way. Keeping a gratitude diary, or making a daily note of your blessings as part of your main journal, will help you see the magic in each day and appreciate the beauty of the world and the hidden moments that often slip by unnoticed. Begin or end each day (or both!) with a list of the things you're grateful for, from the sunshine on your face as you walk in the park to a favour a friend did for you, a new job opportunity, an album you love or some news. There are a million tiny – and not so tiny – things that can bring you joy and a sense of gratitude, and sometimes you just have to pay a bit more attention to start noticing them.

Over the years I've started writing lists of all the things I'm grateful for in my journal, yet despite my best intentions I would eventually give up, pressed for time or some other excuse. But recently a friend started a Facebook group and suggested we post our lists there, and I made a commitment to write down what I was thankful for every day. It's been an amazing experience – I'm constantly surprised by how much you can find to appreciate in a day when you start to look. (Visit www.SereneConneeley.com, and the "With thanks" tab, for examples.)

It's an interesting process. There's been the odd day when I've thought I wouldn't be able to think of anything to write, but once I sit down and try, something always emerges. The nice thing is that it doesn't have to be a massive triumph – sometimes the little things are just as worthy of appreciation. As a result of my daily lists my heart has become flooded with gratitude, and I've started seeing everyday occurrences in a new light, with new appreciation and joy seeping into all parts of my life. This practice has made me seek out the precious little glimmers of happiness and immortalise them so I remember them, has added weight and significance to every moment I experience, and encouraged more magic and more goodness to flow in to my life.

Manifestation Manifesto

Dedicating a journal to your dream, to the thing you most want to make happen in your life, can help you manifest it into reality. To start, write down in colourful, descriptive specifics what you hope to achieve, anchoring it in the physical plane and sending your intention out to the universe. This can be like a manifestation board, with pictures and your favourite motivational quotes stuck in, or a simple list.

Next, write out a detailed plan of how you can make it come true and what you have to do first, which can be updated and fine tuned along the way. Keep track of all the little things you do towards achieving your goal (you'll be surprised how they all add up), and all the things you learn as you progress. Develop affirmations that are personal to you and your dream and repeat and re-read them often, and add stories about other people who have achieved similar things.

Record your emotional journey alongside the physical one, revealing (and releasing) any fears and doubts within the pages of your journal, and offsetting any mini-failures with descriptions of all your triumphs. Write down any flashes of inspiration as they hit you, to re-motivate and re-inspire you when you're feeling discouraged. Like keeping a food or exercise diary, charting your progress in a special journal will encourage you to keep going and help you break things down into manageable chunks so you can make your dream come true.

Divination Diary

If you want to develop your psychic abilities, keeping a diary of daily readings is a great way to begin. Everyone has intuitive powers, but tapping in to them takes practise and patience. Pulling an oracle or tarot card every morning or night and copying its meaning into your journal, as well as meditating on the colourful image and recording your impressions of it in relation to your own situation, will help you learn what the cards signify and rapidly develop your psychic skills.

If you perform a daily reading and record the results for at least a month, significant patterns will begin to emerge, giving you confidence in your abilities and teaching you a lot about oracle work. You'll start to develop your own psychic cues, gain a deeper understanding of symbols and signs, and become a better reader. You can even begin your own dictionary of psychic symbols, with personal meanings to add to the standard ones in the guidebook. And once you feel at home with the deck, you can start doing readings for friends, taking note of the results and their reactions and adding them to your psychic diary.

Exploring any method of divination, be it cards, psychometry, scrying or a pendulum, requires a lot of practise, but you'll be amazed by what you can learn about yourself and how well you can develop your own abilities and connect with your intuition if you do it regularly, recording your results and reflecting on them regularly to discern patterns. Your diary of readings will also provide wisdom, predictions and prophecy about your life, and teach you a lot about who you are, what you want and where you're going. It will provide a fascinating glimpse into the future, as well as offering guidance for dealing with current challenges, giving you insight into your own heart and soul, and deepening your self-reflection even further.

Dream Journal

Recording your dreams and exploring the messages your subconscious sends you while you're sleeping is another way to decode your own wisdom and find solutions to the issues you face. Information, emotions and answers to problems are buried deep within the subconscious, and dreaming allows them to come to the surface of the conscious mind. By recording your nightly dreams, you'll not only see patterns emerging and work out their significance, but also train yourself to remember them better so you can utilise the wisdom they impart.

For the best results, write down your dream as soon as you wake up, even if it's the middle of the night, so you still recall the key moments. If it's easier, you can draw the main points. Then start working out what each symbol means to you and creating your own dream dictionary, because we dream in symbols that have a very personal meaning. A snake could represent wisdom, medical issues or fear depending on how you feel about them, and Angelina Jolie could be telling you something very different depending on whether you perceive her as a humanitarian earth mother, a video game action star or an unscrupulous husband stealer. Dreaming about another person isn't actually about them though; instead they represent an aspect of yourself, and a quality of theirs that you long for or want to release.

Also write down what time you went to bed, what you ate beforehand, what you did and how you felt, because if you dream you're being chased by an axe-wielding murderer after you watched a horror film and gorged on junk food, your dream won't be especially significant, as it's an obvious reaction to what you did that night. Unique nightmares can be very important though, because they often alert you to a problem and allow you to practise how you will respond to it in your waking life. Examine their patterns and delve into their meaning and you'll reveal an emotional issue you need to deal with, and which, once faced, will help you to regain control of your life.

To encourage dreaming, make sure you're not dehydrated and your room isn't too hot. Drink peppermint or rosehip tea before bed and put ash leaves or calendula flowers under your pillow, drawing on the magic of herbal lore to open up your subconscious, then enjoy the wisdom and answers it imparts to you as you sleep. Or place a moonstone next to your bed, as this iridescent, milky crystal illuminated with rainbows increases psychic visions, enhances intuition and sensitivity and boosts dream awareness and spiritual awakening.

Book of Shadows

If you have any interest in witchcraft, you may want to start a Book of Shadows, which charts your personal magical journey. It's a collection of spells, rituals, recipes, goddess chants, pagan symbols, redes, meditations and magical information gained through experience, which is imbued with your own personal energy. While some people now keep their BOS online, a hand-written one has extra power, and is steeped in tradition and history. It's a sacred, often secret book, although in covens they're sometimes passed down and shared around so coven members can reproduce the information into their own.

You can include personal spells you've created as well as favourite ones you've found in books and online – or these can be kept in a separate book called a grimoire if you prefer – plus outlines of rituals you've performed or are planning and detailed records of the outcomes of spellworkings. You can also use your Book of Shadows to record your studies into herbalism, crystals, the elements and other magical subjects, and add sections on the personal meanings of the sabbats and the cycles of the moon. It can include recipes for incense, oils, potions and ritual feasts, old texts, chants and prayers, the results of healing work and divination readings, as well as journal entries about your progress and the unfolding wisdom you are tapping in to.

A Specific Journey

All journals are personal, intimate tools of self-discovery, but dedicating a whole book to exploring one topic can give you even deeper insight into it. You could record your adventures as you start a new job, your experiences throughout a pregnancy or the first year of motherhood, the full moon celebrations and lunar rituals you perform, the details as you settle down in a new city, your healing journey as you deal with an illness, your attempts to learn a new language or master a new skill, memories of your childhood, even the diary of a love affair.

You could also dedicate your journal to a belief you feel really passionately about, be it politics, religion, spirituality, the environment or feminism. Write essays on the topic, getting to the heart of why you care about it and learning to express your opinions eloquently and confidently. Also attempt to argue the opposing view, so you can understand the subject better and have a broader outlook. Include quotes from your favourite thinkers, articles from magazines and reviews of books on the theme, and chart any changes in your thoughts as you come across new information or have new experiences.

Start Your Own Book

Lots of people want to write a book, but they give up before they get anywhere, or never even make a start. Having published two – and started several others I haven't completed yet – I know how very hard it can be to complete a writing project, but also how rewarding it is to finish. Like any goal, the bottom line is that you just have to do it, without making excuses for how busy you are or promising yourself that you'll start next week, next month or next year.

I have a friend who works full-time, does two hours of yoga a day and teaches meditation classes, not to mention suffering through chemo and being hospitalised several times, and she finished her first book in a year. If she can find the time, anyone can! Another friend worked on his novel for just 20 minutes every morning before going to the office, and while it took a while, he got it done.

If you know what you want to write about, start researching the topic. Fill your journal with background information, interviews with case studies or experts, flesh out characters if it's fiction, and scribble down snippets of conversation you hear when you're out if you like the style of. Take your journal with you everywhere and jot down ideas, words, locations and scenarios as they occur to you.

Most importantly, regularly dedicate some time to your writing. It's no surprise that the way to write a book is to sit down and write it. There are no shortcuts, just hard work and dedication to your craft. Children's author Jane Yolen says the "secret" to getting one finished is simple: "Butt in chair. Write something every day – no vacations. My ritual is a cup of tea and fingers on the keyboard, butt in chair."

Famous diarists

"I want to write, but more than that, I want to bring out all kinds of things that lie buried deep in my heart."
Anne Frank, German-born Jewish writer

The power of journalling is reflected in the number of published diaries available, from tales of debauchery by rock bands to the inner workings of a politician's mind. They reveal a desire by the writer not only to be understood by the public, but also to understand themselves, since most are written without any idea that they will one day be published. If you're looking for inspiration, here are some of the most famous of those who journal – Bridget Jones not included…

The Diary of a Young Girl, based on the diaries of Holocaust victim Anne Frank, has been described as one of the wisest and most moving commentaries on war and its impact on humans. In 1933, when Anne was four, her Jewish family fled Germany for Amsterdam because Hitler had come to power. She loved writing stories and wanted to be a writer when she grew up, so she received a diary for her 13th birthday. A few weeks later, with Nazis occupying Holland, she and her family went into hiding in a tiny warehouse space. They remained there for two years, during which Anne wrote every day, until they were discovered and sent to a concentration camp. Anne and her sister died there, but her voice lived on in the diary that was found after her arrest. Anne confided: "When I write, I can shake off all my cares."

For others, a diary is an addiction, a necessary tool to understand themselves and their world. "This diary is my kief, hashish and opium pipe. This is my drug and my vice," said French author Anais Nin, who obsessively kept a journal from the age of 11 until her death in 1977, aged 73. Her many volumes of published diaries explored her life, writing process, erotic imaginings and relationships with fellow authors Henry Miller (and, famously, his wife June), Gore Vidal and Lawrence Durrell, and turned her into a feminist icon in the sixties.

New Zealand writer Katherine Mansfield also kept a series of journals throughout her lifetime, in an attempt to comprehend other people through her own self-realisation. "I want, by understanding myself, to understand others," she explained. Katherine spent the early years of the 20th century in Europe, where she became one of the best short story writers of her generation, and lived a scandalous life alongside friends and fellow literary luminaries DH Lawrence, Virginia Woolf and TS Eliot. After her death in 1923, her estranged husband published her diaries as *The Journal of Katherine Mansfield*, which gives great insight into her life and her work, her emotional struggles and frailties, and the times in which she lived.

Seventeenth century British naval administrator and politician Samuel Pepys is one of the most famous diarists today – his bound volumes, which he wrote from 1660 to 1669, were printed two centuries later, and are today preserved at Cambridge University. These journals, the first to add personal details to the business transactions more commonly recorded, remain one of the most important sources of information about the English Restoration period. His writings were a combination of personal anecdotes, such as life with his wife, his flirtations with other women, his love of wine and his jealousies and how he coped with them, alongside descriptions of significant world events such as London's Great Plague and the Great Fire of 1666.

Eighteenth century English writer Samuel Johnson published the diary of his travels with his friend James Boswell, a Scottish lord and lawyer, as the well-received *Journey to the Western Islands of Scotland*. Following his death, James published his own diary to shed more light on Samuel. In 1816, German philosopher Johann Wolfgang von Goethe released a travel memoir, *Italian Journey*, based on the edited diaries he'd kept as he explored Italy on a pilgrimage seeking knowledge, artistic inspiration and self-awareness. And I referred often to my journals when I was writing *Seven Sacred Sites*, to recall the colour, emotion and numinous beauty of the places I'd visited.

A diary was also the basis of one of the most important books of all time, Charles Darwin's 1859 epic *On the Origin of Species*, which changed forever what the scientific community knows about life itself. Charles, a biologist and geologist who spent five years travelling around the world studying the animals that led him to develop the Theory of Evolution, published the diary of his journey in 1839, which is still in print today as *The Voyage of the Beagle*. In addition to recounting his scientific discoveries, it's also a lush and vividly rendered travel memoir and a portrait of a man searching for truth.

"I've found that keeping a daily journal is a wonderful way to stay in touch with what's important to me and who I want to be."
Bernie Siegel, American doctor and metaphysical writer

I've kept a journal for as long as I can remember, and while there have been times when I've neglected it, it has been an amazing tool of self-discovery, helping to awaken my inner voice and unlock my own innate power and strength. I certainly don't ever want them published, but they've been of immense value to me, reflecting myself back at me so I can identify patterns of behaviour, avoid repeating the same mistakes (eventually!) and learn about who I am, how I feel and what I want.

Because I've always been a bit shy, writing has been the way I've expressed my feelings – most importantly to myself. It's helped me get in touch with my inner world, get to the heart of my emotions and slip beneath the happy facade I put on traumatic events. I write to understand myself, my thoughts and the choices I've made, to remember who I was and who I am, and who I want to be.

Often if I don't journal for a while I feel a bit lost. For me, writing things down allows me to integrate my experiences, good and bad, into my consciousness, and comprehend my life and my self. I gain a unique sense of perspective, and can see the light and shade of life and the cycle of ups and downs that is reassuring in its endless repetition. I know that even in darkness the light will return, because it's happened so many times before. It also fills me with resolve and confidence because I'm reminded of how I handled problems in the past, and how strong I really am. Through keeping a diary and consciously observing my life, I've come to know myself much better.

Writing about your thoughts, emotions, heartbreaks and successes is a great way to get inside your head and unveil the patterns of your actions and reactions. It helps you understand your personality and motivations and make sense of your life, providing insight, freeing your spirit and connecting you to your heart and soul.

Through writing you anchor your emotions, giving form to the overwhelming storm of thoughts and feelings that can sometimes drown you, and bringing your subconscious thoughts into conscious awareness. It shows you what you've missed, reminds you of what you've forgotten and reconnects you to your own true self. Even if you only write a few lines a day, it can provide an amazing snapshot of your life, and be an incredible affirmation of how far you've come.

Keeping a journal develops creativity and intuition, reveals your greatness, your depth and your coping skills, boosts your decision-making processes and makes you happier and more compassionate. It lowers your stress levels, helps you set – and achieve – your goals, organises and focuses you, encourages you to learn and grow, improves your wellbeing and acts as a personal record of your triumphs and tragedies. It also enables you to pause and reflect, to understand who you are and what you really want, and how to go about getting it.

It also gives you a chance to be totally yourself, in the way travelling does, without the weight of other people's expectations. You don't have to edit yourself or limit your thoughts, you can simply express your true self, without judgement. You can spill your biggest dreams, darkest secrets and harshest opinions, and get to know and love the real you.

A diary charts your inner journey and follows your adventures as you connect to your self and become more aware of the yearnings of your heart and soul. It lets you see what you want, believe, hope and dream of, and helps motivate you to make those dreams come true. And by providing insights into your true feelings and emotional depth, it allows you to explore your inner psyche, becoming a powerful expression of your deepest self.

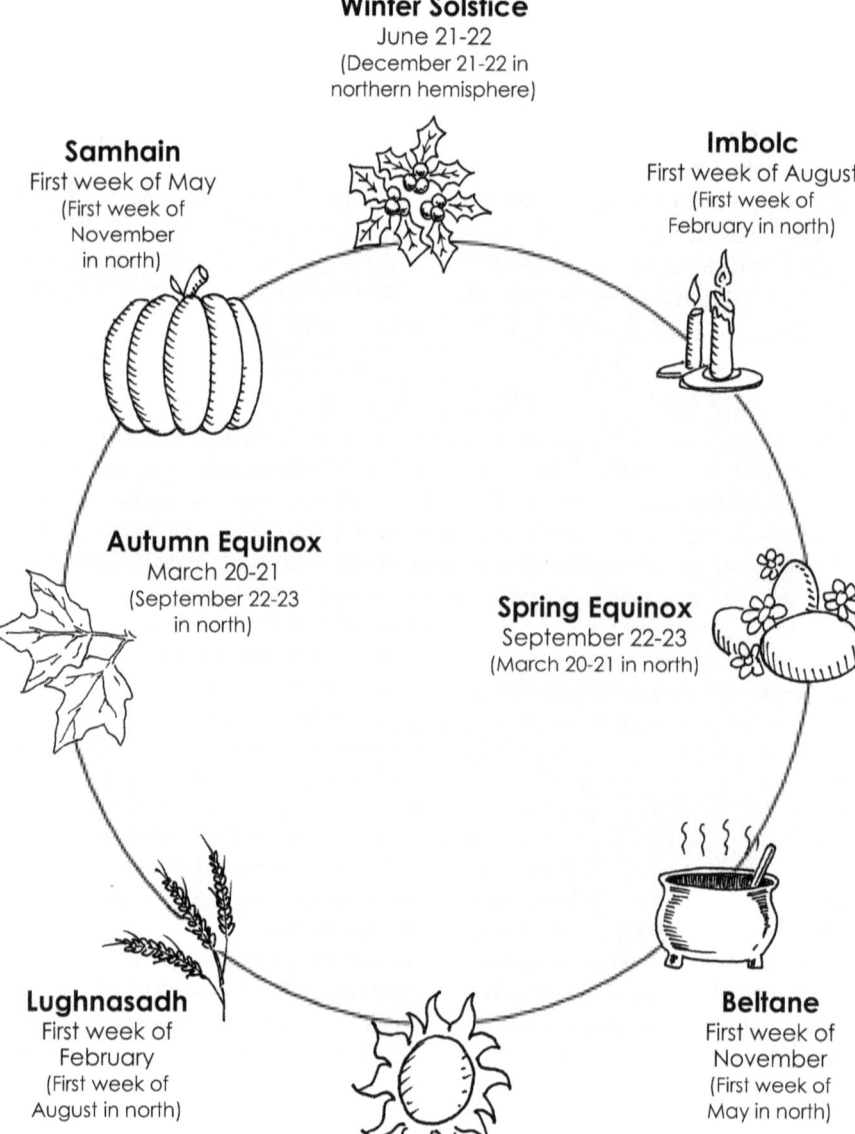

The Magic of the Seasons

"The festivals of the Wheel of the Year are defined by the cycle of nature, by the dance of the weather gods and spirits of place. They require us to look not to the heavens but to the earth. They are set within our soul, watching the leaves on the trees, feeling the shifting temperature and the changing light, within and around."
Emma Restall Orr, British druid priestess, ritualist and author

A powerful way to become more aware of your inner world is to harness the natural magic of the cycles of the seasons. The shifting energies of the earth's turning have been celebrated and utilised for thousands of years, and even today, when we are so far removed from nature, you can still tangibly feel the introspection of winter, the crisp change of autumn, the potent energy of summer and the vibrant power of spring.

Attuning yourself to the vibrations of the eight sacred festivals that make up the enchanted Wheel of the Year will fill you with strength, magic and a sense of grand possibility and potential. You'll become more in sync with yourself and your intuition, and start to connect with your own emotional tides as you connect with the earth's.

These special days, determined by the position of the earth in relation to the sun, mark the beginning, midpoint and end of each season, and are measured today by astronomers and scientists. Long ago they were calculated by the druids, the philosophers and scientists of their age, and recorded in stone circles and cairns. They have been honoured for thousands of years in cultures throughout the world, so the imprint of their energy can be tapped in to and absorbed.

The eight sabbats are a time for celebration and fun, with elaborate rituals being performed and seasonal feasts held to mark the turning of nature and of life. They are also a great time to reflect on your life and where you're at in terms of your emotions, achievements and dreams, so they can be used as part of your journalling process for healing, spiritual development and the manifestation of your goals.

In ages past the Wheel was believed to echo the story of the god and the goddess and their dance of life, love, marriage, death and rebirth, but today it's the symbolic meaning that's most relevant. Planting the seeds of our dreams in the metaphorical spring, watching them grow and manifest in the world during our internal summer, giving thanks for our literal harvest in autumn, allowing the things that no longer serve us to die off or be released in our personal winter, then starting all over again with new dreams as we celebrate our own rebirth and continue the magical cycle of the seasons and of life.

Yule : Winter Solstice : Rebirth

The winter solstice falls around June 21 or 22 in the southern hemisphere and December 21 or 22 in the northern hemisphere. It's the longest night and the shortest day of the year, and marks the transition between darkness and light, both literally and metaphorically, as well as emotionally and physically.

Mythologically, this was when the goddess gave birth to the sun god, who was reborn as an infant and began to grow towards manhood, reaching full strength six months later at the summer solstice. It represented the return of the light, and the life force, to the world.

Astronomically, this solstice – which comes from the Latin word solstitium, from sol (sun) and sistere (to stand still) – occurs when the sun is as far north as it goes, or, in the northern hemisphere, as far south, before it turns and heads back towards the Equator. At the time of the winter solstice in the southern hemisphere, the sun will be overhead the Tropic of Cancer, making it Midsummer in the north. At Midwinter in the northern hemisphere, the sun is above the Tropic of Capricorn, the furthest latitude south it reaches.

Of course it's the earth that moves in relation to the sun, not vice versa, but it's much easier to imagine the sun moving through the sky, alternating above each hemisphere as it creates our seasons. During the winter solstice in the southern hemisphere, the South Pole is tilted away from the sun, at its most extreme angle (around 23.5°), so the sun's rays are less intense and the southern lands receives less daylight and warmth, while their northern counterparts receive their day of greatest light.

The winter solstice, also known as Midwinter, Yule, Alban Arthan (the light of the bear), Wassail, the Winter Rite, Festival of Dionysus, Saturnalia and Birth of the Sun, marks the middle of winter, and in most parts of the world it's cold, bleak and wet, even snowing, at this time. It's the lowest point of the Wheel in terms of energy and light, with the sun rising later and night falling earlier.

This is a quiet, reflective time – animals hide away to hibernate, seeds lie underground, closed up and cold, and nature withdraws so it can rest in order to regain its strength before it begins to regenerate. Energetically people feel tired and unmotivated too, more inclined to snuggle up on the couch with a good book or go to bed early than to leap up and take action to pursue their dreams.

Winter is for rest and reflection, conserving your energy and acknowledging sadness and loss – of dreams, of friendships, of parts of your self. It's a good time to work with the element of water, which is associated with emotions, cleansing and letting go. Stand outside in the rain, arms outstretched to the sky and face gazing upwards, and let the water wash away any fears, regrets, sadness or painful memories. There's something so liberating about being outside in the wildness of a storm and letting the elements wash away all that you want to let go of, but you could also dive into the ocean or soak in a scented bath to feel yourself symbolically cleansed and reborn.

Metaphorically, the energy of this season supports washing away what is no longer necessary and creating a fertile base from which to move forward. Get in touch with the things you want to change in your life, whether it's finding a new job, meeting someone, moving house or transforming your spiritual life, and let go of anything that no longer serves you. You can't achieve your goals until you're certain of what they are, so listen to your inner voice and pay attention to the feelings you've long buried so you can focus on what's important.

The bleakness of winter can cause depression, doctors have found, with seasonal affective disorder now a recognised medical condition. A touch of the winter blues is not uncommon because sunlight affects brain chemistry, and its lack can impact on your wellbeing.

But the winter solstice is a day of hope, the turning point in this time of darkness, introspection and dreaming. Considered the dark night of the soul that gives birth to the creative spark, it marks the point where the dark half of the year relinquishes its hold to the light half. After this longest night, the days will slowly start to lengthen, the strength of the sun will slowly increase, and the energy, within and without, will slowly begin to build.

The midwinter festival is about the re-emergence of light from the dark, so it is a celebration of the earth's – and our – renewal. It's the perfect time to examine and acknowledge your potential and start dreaming of all the things you want to achieve. This is a day of rebirth, transformation and healing, a time to nurture yourself, and to rest and relax in preparation for the rush of growth in the spring.

Ways to celebrate

In the northern hemisphere the winter solstice celebration of Yule coincides with the modern season of Christmas, whose traditions were borrowed from the ancient solstice festivities. Pagans had marked this day with feasting, gift giving and candle-lit trees for centuries before the coming of Christ, honouring the goddess as she gave birth to the sun god, welcoming the sun, and celebrating the turning of the wheel of life from the barrenness and death in the fields to the rebirth of the crops promised by the lengthening days.

In Ancient Egypt at this time they celebrated the birth of Horus, son of the goddess Isis, with partying, feasts and presents; the Persians maintained fires all night to honour their solar god, protect the sun and keep the forces of darkness at bay; and in Ancient Rome, the solstice celebration called Sol Invictus, the Day of the Unconquered

Sun, took place, which honoured the birth of their sun god Mithras, the saviour who brought light to their world.

But with the spread of Christianity this day of light and transformation was turned into Christmas, to take the spotlight off the sun god and put it on to the son of God. In 350CE, Pope Julius I declared that Christ's birth would be celebrated on December 25, to make it as painless as possible for the pagan Romans, who remained a majority at that time, to convert to the new religion.

All the same traditions continued, traditions that live on today in the Christmas tree that's decorated at this time, the presents we put under it, the huge family meals we cook and the recognition of the birth of the son of God as opposed to the sun god.

To mark the solstice and absorb the energy of the season, decorate an evergreen tree, which symbolises the hope of spring's return. Even in the dead of winter these trees remain green, filled with nature's life force, which makes them a potent symbol of fertility and vitality. Pine trees were common – and remain popular – because they represent life, potency and rebirth, as so many trees can grow from a single cone.

Have a Yule feast, inviting your friends over to celebrate and exchange little presents. Pots of herbs such as chamomile, rosemary and comfrey, and plants such as sunflower, ivy and elder, encapsulate the magic and energy of the season. Decorate your home with pine cones and sprigs of mistletoe and holly, and drape the table in a red, green or gold cloth, with candles in the same colours.

If you have a fireplace, burn the traditional Yule log (usually pine or oak), lighting it at dusk and letting it burn through the night to welcome back the sun. Keep a little of the burned log to start your fire next year, and collect the ashes of the sacred wood for healing spells and rituals, as they embody the life-giving powers of the sun.

Stay up all night, celebrating, laughing and sharing your plans for the future, then go outside as morning approaches to welcome the first rays of the sun. Toast the dawn, honour the corresponding dawning of your own potential, and give thanks for this energetic reawakening. Or you may prefer to make it a solitary celebration and inner journey, going within with a solo ritual or journalling session to embody the energy of the sabbat on a deeper, more personal level.

In the southern hemisphere, the winter solstice falls in June, six months before Christmas, which can make things a bit confusing. But there is increasing awareness in Australia and other Down Under countries that Christmas is based on magical winter traditions, and many festive-themed events, such as the Winter Magic Festival, Yulefest and Hollyfrost, are now held in the correct season, in recognition that the winter solstice celebration of Yule should not take place in December, in the heat of the southern summer, but in the cool and introspective months of winter.

In your journal

This festival of hope and renewal is the perfect time to reflect on the past year, to acknowledge the good and the bad, the dreams you fulfilled and the ones you let die, and the things you still hope to achieve. In the northern hemisphere New Year's Eve is approaching, and people contemplate the end of one year and the start of the next, which fits perfectly with the seasonal energy.

Start by reviewing your past 12 months. If you've been keeping a journal, re-read it, then summarise the high and low points, pondering how much you have changed, how much you achieved, and where you're at now compared to last winter. If you haven't kept a written record, just let your memory drift, and make notes of the events and emotions you recall. If you start feeling nostalgic and introspective, dive right into it and embrace the recollections.

This is a time for nurturing your heart and soul, listening to its wisdom, tapping in to the subconscious thoughts that have been buried and learning the lessons of the past so you can emerge from your wintry cocoon into the new light and energy to come. You're preparing your soul's fertile ground for the seeds you'll soon plant, by drawing on the richness you already have deep within.

This solstice is also a good time to be still and quiet, to look inside your heart and soul and ponder the Mysteries. It's important for your own wellbeing and peace of mind to allow such introspection and self-examination, to let yourself slow down and decide what it is you really want, otherwise you may find yourself pursuing a goal that isn't yours or a dream you no longer care about.

At this time of year, in the middle of winter, the land appears to be dormant or even dead, yet it's not – it's simply awaiting the touch of the sun to bring it back to life. Likewise you are filled with the seeds of your dreams, and need only recognise them and acknowledge them, and shine the light of your inner strength on them, to awaken and invigorate them. The solstice is a great time to work out what it is you want to achieve, and start outlining in broad strokes the ways to do so.

Light a gold or yellow candle on Midwinter's Eve to symbolise the sun and its activating energy, and breathe in its vibration and light as you stare into the flame and focus on your dreams for the coming year. Open yourself up to the promise of new growth and achievement, the energy of renewal and the rebirth of your own self and creativity as the sun is also reborn.

Symbolically and energetically it's a time to honour your inner wisdom, consider the lessons you learned during winter's introspection and integrate them into your life so you can start to initiate change. And have patience with yourself. There is a regenerative power in stillness, in preparing and being rested and ready for when the energy of growth and productivity of springtime returns.

Imbolc: First Day of Spring: Purification

Imbolc, the festival of joy and renewal that marks the end of winter and the start of spring, falls in the first week of August in the southern hemisphere, and the first week of February in the northern hemisphere. It celebrates the fact that the days are lengthening and the light is returning, illuminating the land as well as our own hearts.

Mythologically, this was when the goddess transformed back into the maiden and waiting bride, after the crone energy of winter, signified by the new blossoms and unfurling buds and the quickening energy within the earth, while the infant god continued to grow in power, represented by the longer days and increasing strength of the sun.

Astronomically, this cross-quarter day falls midway between the winter solstice and the spring equinox. In the southern hemisphere, it occurs when the sun is halfway between the Tropic of Cancer and the Equator on its journey back from the north, and it rises in the same position as it did at Samhain, when it was heading up towards the north from the Equator for its Midwinter sun stand still.

Imbolc, also known as Candlemas, Oimelc, the Snowdrop Festival, Lupercus, Gwyl Fair, the Feast of Pan, Bridie's Day and Brigantia (the Festival of Brigid), signifies the first day of spring. Signs of winter's end appear – the first tentative flowers bloom, ice and snow melt and the sun strengthens, symbolising the return and renewal of the life force of the land and its people. Imbolc was the first of three fertility festivals on the agricultural calendar, and the name is believed to come from the Irish word for in the womb, because sheep were pregnant and swelling with new life at this time. It can also be linked to the word oimelc, or ewe's milk, while others claim the name comes from a similar word that meant purification, which all fit in with the seasonal energy of budding new life that this day celebrates.

Energetically it's a time of awakening, renewal and re-emergence, as nature fills with life force and begins to quiver with the energy to grow again, and we too start to emerge from the chill of winter, shaking off our inertia and lack of motivation and beginning to re-engage with the world. It's also a time of purification and cleansing after the long dark of the winter months, of stripping away the old so the new can emerge. Imbolc is one of the four fire festivals of the year, and great bonfires would be lit not only in celebration but also for purification, so cleansing has always been an important aspect of the day.

People would ritually purify themselves to let go of the darkness and sluggishness of the hibernation of winter, making it a time of spiritual renewal. They would also clean their home, physically and energetically, to assist their inner purification – the modern tradition of spring cleaning on the first day of spring reflects this ancient practice. It's a good time to clean out your home, office and wardrobe, and energetically clear your space, sweeping out old energy – and old thoughts – so the new can thrive. And if you want to begin a new spiritual practise, be it meditation, automatic writing, chanting, chakra therapy or yoga, the energy of this time will aid you.

Imbolc is a festival of light, celebrating the return of the sun and its life-giving warmth. It is dedicated to Bridie, the maiden fire goddess, whose transformative flames help purify and burn away doubt and pain. Bridie, also known as Bridget and Bride, was associated with inspiration and creativity, making it a great day to express your inner muse. She was also linked with intuition, and because the ancients believed that the veil between the worlds was thinner on the cross-quarter days, she was invoked for assistance with divination rituals and prophecy at this time, including weather prognostication.

The Celts watched the native wildlife for signs that winter was over. In addition to plants sprouting, it was believed that if creatures such as badgers and serpents popped their heads out of their barrow at Imbolc and saw their shadow, which would startle them and send them back underground, spring was still a way off, but if they popped up and it was overcast, so there was no shadow and they stayed outside, it signified that winter was over. Groundhog Day, which is celebrated at Imbolc in North America, is based on this old pagan tradition.

Ways to celebrate

Imbolc remains a day to honour the fertility of the land and your self. As the first signs of spring start to manifest, and the earth quickens with an energy that can be tangibly felt, it's also a powerful time to do healing work of any kind, and send energy to friends around the world. And you can increase your knowledge in an area you're interested in, expand your creativity and tend to activities that are overlooked in the busy months of summer – making candles, sewing dream pillows, grinding herbs and blessing the seeds you'll plant in spring.

All over the world the coming of spring is celebrated as a time of hope, renewal and fresh starts after winter's slowness. In Japan, the Shinto spring festival of Setsubun is celebrated on February 3, recognised there as the first day of spring. Special purification rituals are performed to cleanse away the negativity of the old year and allow the new to blossom into life, and beans are thrown to deter bad spirits.

Chinese New Year is also a spring festival that ushers in new energy and transformation. To absorb its spirit, spring clean your home, throwing out any tired reminders of the old year to make space for the good fortune of the new year to enter. Burn sage sticks or perform a house blessing ritual to clear any negative energies that have settled inside during winter, have a ritual bath and drink cleansing herb teas and plenty of water with a squeeze of lemon to detoxify your body.

As the flowers begin to blossom after winter's chill, weave a wreath of primroses, dandelions and other spring blooms to wear in your hair, or plant these flowers in your garden to call on the energy and life force of the season. Make Bridie Crosses with stalks of wheat or pipe cleaners to hang around the house as symbols of the goddess and of protection. Light candles and set them in all your windows and throughout the house, then burn white or pale blue candles for your ritual – or simply for your dinner table – to embody the innocence and purity of the day, and represent the purifying power of the element of fire.

For thousands of years, Imbolc has been celebrated with rituals involving the lighting of candles and fires to represent the return of the warmth and light and the slowly increasing power of the sun. To absorb this fire energy, perform some candle magic. Light a white or gold candle and stare into the flame as you concentrate on what you want, then blow it out, sending your desire out to the universe. Making a wish as you blow out the candles on your birthday cake is a magic that has survived from pagan times, and is a potent way to manifest your dreams into reality, whatever day it is.

If you want to hold a simple ritual with friends, sit in a circle, each with a tealight candle. One person lights their candle as they make a wish or a statement of intent, then the next person ignites theirs from the one that is already lit, going around the circle in a deosil (with the sun) direction, which is anti-clockwise in the southern hemisphere, until you have a vibrant ring of fire. The last person should light a large central candle with their tealight, which will absorb and hold the magic of the group and can be lit whenever you are together again.

You can also hold a candle-making party, infusing each waxwork creation with your personal energy, or give everyone a floating candle, light them and set them adrift on a pond or pool, or just in a bowl of water, sending your intentions out into the universe and calling on the magic of all the elements to help you make them come true. Bridie is also associated with sacred wells, so combining the elements of fire and water in this way helps you further absorb her archetypal energy.

Like most pagan festivals, the Church superimposed its own holiday over Imbolc. It turned the festival of the goddess Bridie into the feast day of Saint Bridget, a figure also associated with the sacred flame. To temper the significance of the pagan candle ceremonies, they declared the next day Candlemas, the day the priests bless the church candles. And in the Roman Empire, where candlelight processions in honour of Juno, the goddess of marriage, were held on this day, the Pope created a holy day, the Purification of the Blessed Virgin, marked with a candle ceremony, to honour the day they decided Mary became "clean" again 40 days after giving birth. Each of these new celebrations still incorporated the old traditions of purification, cleansing and fire, so the seasonal associations remained, hidden within the new religion.

In your journal

Imbolc is a time of young, innocent love, so try to see yourself, and the world, through the pure eyes of a child, or a child-like heart, with joy and hope. It's a festival of spiritual renewal and inspiration, so it's a good time to write about your beliefs and examine how you feel about your spiritual path, exploring the reasons you think the way you do and perhaps questioning if there are other viewpoints you might also embrace. It's also about new beginnings, and in some magical traditions it is the day chosen for initiations and rededications, so if you want to make a pledge to a new path or a new goal, or a personal vow of any kind, you will be supported by the energy of the season.

Another major theme of Imbolc is purification, so after cleaning your home physically, start to focus on the concept of emotional clearing. Shrug off any old energies or old ideas that are holding you back. If a person or situation is bothering you, write about it, purging yourself of all the "negative" emotions you're holding within your body, which can affect you physically if you suppress them.

If you can't release them, write a few words or draw a symbol that represents the issue and put it in the freezer. This will put your angst on ice, so to speak, and stop the problem affecting you. It won't alter what's going on or influence anyone else involved, or their actions, but it will change the way you feel about it and prevent it from upsetting you any further. To add potency, put the piece of paper in an ice cube tray, fill it with water and add a little honey to sweeten the situation, a drop of rose water to bring love to all the parties involved, a drop of orange oil for happiness, or a sprig of basil to improve communication.

Most importantly, as this is the festival of Bridie, the goddess of healing and inspiration, it's the perfect day to unleash your inner muse and connect with your creativity. Talk to Bridie – or Saint Bridget, or the higher self aspect of yourself – or write a letter, and express all the things you want to create in the next 12 months.

Write down any answers you receive or any impressions that flood your mind. Meditate on these goals and record what comes up for you. Don't worry about how to achieve them, as that will be revealed later as flashes of inspiration, guidance or outside help. Just write your truths and your inner feelings, channelling the inspiration that fills you, without editing or controlling what you reveal to yourself.

Take special note of your dreams too, and add them to your journal so you can start to see any patterns that your psyche is trying to reveal and identify the deeper meanings of the symbols within them. Bridie was also the patron of poetry, so express yourself in verse too, letting your subconscious thoughts bubble to the surface and your inspiration run wild. This is a time of affirmation and manifestation, so make sure every thought you have and every word you write is positive and full of love for yourself and the universe.

Ostara : Spring Equinox : Blossoming

The spring equinox is celebrated around September 22 or 23 in the southern hemisphere, and March 20 or 21 in the northern hemisphere. At this point night and day are of equal length, and it's a time of balance and harmony both within and without.

Mythologically, this was when the young god reached maturity and became the lover-consort of the maiden goddess. In some traditions it marked their sexual union, and the conceiving of the child that would be born nine months later at the winter solstice; in others it was when the goddess began instructing the god in his new powers. It was also when the harvest deity Demeter was reunited with her daughter Persephone, who'd been kidnapped by Hades and, having eaten six pomegranate seeds while she was in the underworld, was now bound to spend six months of each year there. She went down at the autumn equinox, and her mother made the earth barren, then she re-emerged in the spring, when Demeter brought the land back to life again.

Astronomically, this equinox – Latin for equal night – is one of only two times in the year that the length of day and night is the same, as the sun sits directly above the Equator, creating 12 hours of light and 12 hours of dark in each hemisphere. It represents the triumph of light over dark, because for the next six months, until the autumn equinox, the days will be longer than the nights.

The spring equinox, also known as the vernal equinox (from the Latin vernare, to bloom), Ostara, Eostre, Lady Day, Earrach, Alban Eiler (light of the earth) and the Festival of Trees, marks the midpoint of spring. It's a celebration of fertility, conception and regeneration as the earth begins to bloom and the memory of winter's harshness fades away. It's a time of new growth, where all of nature seems to be sprouting and blossoming. Seedlings emerge from the earth, new crops are sown, the buds on the trees open, birds build nests and lay eggs, and new life and momentum is celebrated.

Energetically, the spring equinox is a time of emergence and vitality. Life force courses through the planet, as well as through us. People throw off the dreariness of the cold months and awaken physically and mentally. Exercise and activity becomes easier, and motivation returns. This is the time to sow the seeds of what you want to achieve in the coming year, blessing them with your energy and intent, and to dedicate yourself to new goals. The vibration of this season supports the blossoming and growth of your personality, your spiritual and emotional development, and your dreams. It's a very fertile time, when you can make things happen and create your own reality.

This equinox is about growth, passion and the unfurling and release of the immense potential you have within you. On both a universal and a personal level, it's a time of balance and harmony, of union between the physical and the spiritual, and the integration of your heart and soul. This can be harnessed to anchor your dreams in reality and enhance your own inner harmony as the balance of universal outer energies is reflected within.

Ways to celebrate

Traditionally the spring equinox was a time of resurrection, as life returned throughout nature. The leaves on the trees were budding, flowers blossoming, crops sprouting, birds and animals mating. Thanks was given to Ostara, the goddess of fertility, the dawn and spring, whose symbols were an egg and a hare, and who is still honoured around the world, albeit unknowingly, in the form of chocolate eggs and the bunnies that have come to evoke Easter, the Christian festival of resurrection. In the northern hemisphere Easter takes place around Ostara – it's the first Sunday after the full moon on or after the spring equinox – so for pagans there it's easy to celebrate this sabbat as the symbols of springtime are everywhere, on cards and supermarket shelves and even in ads and TV shows. In the south however Easter coincides with the autumn equinox and harvest rituals, and Ostara and the blossoming of spring occurs in September, when the chocolate eggs are long gone.

Eggs have represented new life, spring, fertility and the cycle of rebirth for thousands of years. In Ancient Rome and Persia people exchanged them as gifts, wrapped in gold leaf or boiled with flower petals to colour them, to celebrate spring and the new year. They've long been associated with the goddess too, with the yellow yolk symbolising the sun god and the egg white the maiden goddess, who were believed to come together at this time. Even the *Catholic Encyclopedia* admits the custom has its origin in paganism: "For a great many pagan customs celebrating the return of spring gravitated to Easter. The egg is the emblem of the germinating life of early spring."

The other symbol, the hare, has signified abundance, life force, good fortune and fertility (due to its prolific breeding habits, hence the term "breeding like rabbits"!) from Ancient Egypt to Great Britain to China. The march hare was so named because it was nocturnal for most of the year, but in March in the northern hemisphere its mating season began and the creatures were outside all day, leaping around joyously in search of a mate. The females are incredibly fertile, able to conceive another litter of bunnies while still pregnant with the first, and birthing up to 42 offspring a year. The males are also very fertile, and very keen – if they're rebuffed they perform a crazy dance to try to impress the female, giving rise to the phrase: "Mad as a march hare."

Springtime is all about fertility, rebirth and renewal, so to absorb the energy of the season, paint some hard-boiled eggs and decorate them with symbols that represent your desires, or make some chocolate eggs, meditating on your own metaphorical fertility and your ability to manifest your dreams into reality as you do so. Gift some to your friends, wishing them success in their own endeavours, or display them on your altar or your breakfast table.

Go outside during the day and breathe in the fresh spring air, filling your heart with new inspiration as you fill your lungs with oxygen. Walk around your neighbourhood and check out all the beautiful flowers that are blooming, and become aware of the energy coursing up from the earth. Feel it reinvigorate and inspire you, flooding you with a sense of renewal and fresh starts. Wear flowers in your hair or perfume scented with jasmine, roses or violets. Plant a seed or a tree in your garden or just in a pot in the kitchen, infusing it with your intent and determination. Then nurture it along, seeing your own progress symbolically reflected in its growth.

In many cultures, including that of the Ancient Romans, whose calendar ours is based on, and the modern Iranians, who use the old Persian calendar, the spring equinox is the first day of the year, with its attendant sense of hope, optimism and new beginnings. In Japan, the springtime Cherry Blossom Festival takes place, while in India, Nepal and several other eastern countries the spring festival of Holi is held, which celebrates the season of growth and new life with rituals to ensure the blessings of the gods for good harvests and fertility.

Welcome this energy of rebirth into your life by spring cleaning your home. Sort through your closets, clean out the kitchen cupboards, organise your office and go through your garage. Let go of what you don't need, giving it to charity, to friends or posting it on eBay. Decluttering is a key principle of the ancient science of feng shui, which balances the energy of your environment to enhance your life and promote health, wealth and happiness. Possessions you no longer need, use or want weigh you down and literally drain you of energy and motivation. In clearing clutter you're inviting transformation to occur, and opening the way for positive new opportunities to enter your life. You'll be flooded with new ideas, meet new people and feel more energised and positive about everything in your life.

In your journal

Spring is the growing season, so celebrate it by connecting with the energy of growth. Plant the seeds of the things you want to achieve in the coming year, which means being clear and taking action to make what you want happen. Crops don't grow unless you sow the seeds, and dreams don't come true until you work to make them happen.

It's amazing how many people talk about how desperate they are to do something, yet they never start. Even the wildest dream can be achievable if you break it down into little steps and patiently work towards it. Detail your plan in your journal, writing about what you actually seek and the specifics of what it involves and requires. Outline the first action you need to take, and the next – and then start today.

If you want a new job, rewrite your resume and send it to companies you want to work for, or sign up for a course that will qualify you for the career you aspire to. If you want to travel, open a savings account and set up an automatic payment plan today, and research the countries you long to visit. If you want to meet a partner, write a list of the qualities you seek and the things you don't want, focusing on what you want to manifest. Deal with any issues you have from past relationships and let go of bitterness, anger and regret. Forgive your exes, and yourself. Make your own happiness your priority, because when you're the best person you can be – content, at peace, doing what you want to do – you'll attract someone with the same qualities, be it a romantic partner, business colleague or a friend.

The equinox is about harmony and balance, so it's a good time for unions, partnerships and initiations, both with others and with all the parts of yourself. Do a ritual or simply write in your journal about all the subtleties and shades of your character, the positive and the so-called negative, and integrate and accept all of them.

To find balance involves an acceptance of all aspects of the inner self – your protective side and your nurturing side, the aggressive and the gentle, the masculine and the feminine. Many people deny a part of themselves, afraid to be considered too emotional or too driven, too girlie or too tough, but getting in touch with your true self and all aspects of your personality is crucial to being the best and most effective person you can be, to achieving your dreams and finding true love and contentment.

Spring is also a time of newness and fresh starts, so let go of any mistakes you're obsessing over and wipe your slate clean. Write about any situations you regret, being honest about the part you played and looking for any lesson you can take from it, then release it. Scribble down a word or draw a symbol to represent the event, then light a green candle and burn the paper in its flame, feeling the vibration of the wasted emotion or past incident leaving your body and your mind, and embracing the energy of a new start, a new future, a new dream. Ostara is the goddess of the dawn as well as fertility, and symbolises the dawning of a new day and all the potential and promise inherent in that. Make a resolution that reflects this new start, and feel its energy and power as you begin afresh.

In the coming months, re-read your journal at regular intervals and be re-inspired and re-motivated to keep aiming for your dream. Go over the plan you outlined above and reassess how you're progressing. Like a little seedling breaking through the earth, you need to nurture, protect and guide the progress of your goals.

Beltane: First Day of Summer: Growth

Beltane, the festival of love and fertility that marks the end of spring and the start of the heat and energy of summer, falls in early November in the southern hemisphere and early May in the northern hemisphere. It's the third fertility festival of the year, and celebrates the fact that the days are continuing to lengthen and the temperature is increasing.

Mythologically, this was when the god and the goddess were balanced in power and age, when they were lovers and equals. It was a time of sexual union – in some magical traditions it was the day the goddess conceived; while in others it was when she married the god.

Astronomically, this cross-quarter day occurs midway between the spring equinox and the summer solstice. In the southern hemisphere, the sun is halfway between the Equator and the Tropic of Capricorn on its journey towards the southernmost latitudes, and rises in the same position as it does three months later at Lughnasadh, when it's heading back north to the Equator.

Beltane, also known as Bealtaine (bright fire), May Day, Walpurgis Night, the Festival of Flowers and Floralia, marks the first day of summer. The evidence of new life is everywhere, in abundant blossoms, the hatching of birds, and bees pollinating flowers. The seeds planted in spring have germinated and sprouted, and the land is warm, buzzing and green. Brightly coloured flowers were traditionally brought inside to symbolise fresh beginnings and the power of nature, and pretty white blossoms were gathered from the sacred hawthorn tree, which was associated with Beltane and used for love spells, in marriage rituals, to make wands as well as for protection and healing. Women would also bathe their faces in the dew gathered from their garden on Beltane morning to harness the energy of youth.

At the four cross-quarter days the veil between the worlds is considered to be thinner, and at this one people connected with the energy of the fairies, who were believed to emerge into the human world on this night to dance, find a lover, impart their wisdom and teach the odd lesson before withdrawing back into the mists.

Beltane was the major fertility festival of the Celtic year, and lovers would leap over bonfires hand in hand to renew their vows of love, then come together in sacred union in the fields to bless the crops with fertility. Maypole dancing, representing the union of the god (the pole) and the goddess (the ribbons), was performed to join the two forces of masculine and feminine, and May Day was, and still is, one of the most popular days for marriages in the northern hemisphere.

But in the southern hemisphere the Beltane festivities fall in early November, which coincides with Samhain/Halloween. While some pagans don witch, vampire or ghost costumes for trick or treat parties at this time, they're just as likely to dress as fairies and wood nymphs to represent the gentle, bright and light fae energy and the vitality and heat of the season, and perform rituals to boost love and fertility.

The festival of Beltane, no matter when it is celebrated, is a time of sunshine and abundant growth, of lovers and spells to attract love, and of celebrating the fertility of life, not just physically, but also of our dreams and ambitions and creativity.

Ways to celebrate

Beltane is a celebration of summer and of life, fertility and joy. In Ancient Rome it was called the Floralia, and was a flower festival in honour of Flora, their goddess of plants and nature. It was believed that she caused the trees, flowers and crops to grow, and also brought to fruition the blossoming of the human heart.

Hers was a sensuous festival, with rituals, games, erotic dancing, theatre performances, flower-clad altars and people swathed in colourful robes and ribbons. Golden torches lit up the night so the revelry could continue until dawn, and people abandoned themselves joyously to the rites. Legend recalls that Flora had a magic flower that would make any woman who touched it fall pregnant, which ties in with the energies of the Celtic festival as well, which was all about the fertility of the earth, the animals and humanity.

As the land thrummed and surged with energy and growth, and flowers bloomed and sap rose within the trees, people also felt the wildness of nature. The Green Man, the spirit of nature, was honoured at this time, along with Cernunnos, the horned god and deity of Beltane and the summer. Many children were conceived at this time, and the Great Rite, also called the Sacred Marriage, was performed, which symbolised the joining of god and goddess. Re-enacting this ceremony, which people believed created the universe, reassured them that life would go on. It also united the two forces of masculine and feminine and the elements of yin and yang that were so central to nature-based religions.

The Great Rite was consummated literally, with a priestess playing the goddess and representing mother earth, and a priest embodying the god. At other times it was the king, who had to wed the land to retain his royal power, who channelled the god and joined with the goddess. This rite ensured the fertility of the land, and is still performed today in many magical traditions, although for most it is done symbolically, not literally, with a ritual involving a chalice and athame.

Huge bonfires were lit on Beltane Eve, which represented fertility, purification and healing, and burned through the night. Cattle were driven between them to be cleansed on their way out to the summer fields, and the fires were also the focus of Beltane celebrations, with dancing and revelry continuing around them all night. Couples leaped over them together as a vow of commitment, to bring luck to their union and to publicly pledge their love to each other, and the ceremony represented a contract of marriage for a year and a day.

This energy makes it a wonderful time to repledge your love to your partner. You don't have to build a bonfire and leap over it, although you can! Simply lighting a red or gold candle as you stare into each other's eyes and speak your love and commitment is enough to invoke the power and passion of the element of fire. If you're single, make a commitment of some kind to yourself, nurture a friendship or sing your intention and your wanting of a romantic partner to the universe.

Love spells are also performed at this time, to take advantage of the universal energies swirling around. It can be as simple as lighting a pink candle and making a wish, holding a rose quartz as you list the qualities you long for in a partner or soaking in a bath filled with pink rose petals, or it can be as involved as you want to make it, with moon phases and invocations and a lengthy list of ingredients. Just don't cast it on anyone specific, as this contradicts the witchie principle of never interfering with someone's free will – and you could end up binding a psycho to you and having trouble getting free!

Instead add a little magic to your life by empowering yourself, increasing your confidence and your attitude. If you want to draw a partner to you, don't go for a specific person, just focus on manifesting someone with the qualities you desire, as there may be someone you don't know yet who is perfectly suited. This is why spells often end with: "This or something better..." because you don't want to limit yourself just to the possibilities you can imagine. So, put your desire out to the universe, and trust that the perfect person will respond.

Beltane is also considered the festival of the fairies, and during the long, bright evenings of early summer you can almost see them dancing in your garden, flitting from vivid coloured flower to gently waving leaf. You can connect to the energy of the day by opening up to the fairy realm. Paint, draw, write about or hang pictures of these magical winged beings, or perform a divination reading with a fairy oracle deck, drawing on their wisdom to gain insight into your future and any issues you are facing. Dress up in long, swirling clothes with flowers in your hair and dance barefoot on the grass, soaking up the vibration of the earth and of this powerful, potent time. The magic and beauty of the fae's archetypal energy stirs something deep within and touches the heart, bringing joy and inspiration, while their vibration can alter ours and bring lightness to the soul.

In your journal

Beltane is all about fertility, both literally and metaphorically. Symbolically this day marks the igniting of the fires of creativity and passion, and the fertility of your dreams being made manifest. Embrace this energy and do all that you can to nurture and further your goals, because any form of action will be supported at this time. Check in on the projects you started at the spring equinox, and write about their progress and the ways in which they've sprouted into reality. If you need to fine tune anything, learn a new skill or simply let go of an aspect so it can germinate further on its own, now is a good time.

At Beltane, when the god and the goddess are equals, neither mother and child nor maiden and wise old sage, aim to rebalance the masculine and feminine energies within yourself. Make sure you give equal power to your gentle, intuitive, feminine side as you do to your more outgoing, active, masculine side. This has nothing to do with gender, but simply the myriad aspects of your deeper self. Most people overlook, bury or neglect one side of themselves at times, but both are crucial to feeling loved, loveable and loving.

This is a festival of passion – passion for life, for love, for your dreams – so revel in whatever you feel most passionate about. Celebrate the fertility of life by conceiving new ideas, or do some word association in your journal until you stumble upon a plan or a goal that fills you with joy. Begin a new project, sign up for a course or start a new hobby, knowing that the universe is bursting with raw energy and power that you can tap in to simply by breathing it in.

It's also a day of love, so it's a good time to focus on self-love. Start writing a list of all the qualities and attributes you love about yourself, and all the reasons you are so loveable and so worthy of love. If it gets hard, take a deep breath and keep going, as it means this is an important exercise for you. (I still find this one hard, and have lots of pauses and struggles and fears and tears when I do it, but it's worth persevering with.) Sit within a sacred space and light a white candle for innocent love, a pink candle for pure love and a red candle for passionate love. Focusing on each in turn, write something positive about yourself that fits with that energy. Let the fire of the flame take you deeper inside yourself so you can connect to your essence and see yourself as you truly are, with all your kindness, your beauty, your caring and your light brought to the surface.

The Beltane fires aren't only for couples – they can be jumped over alone or with friends as part of a personal ritual of purification and preparation, leaping out of your past, burning away the relationship issues that have kept your heart closed, and towards a future where love is possible. You can do this symbolically, stepping over a candle flame rather than a fire, as you let go of all the old, false thoughts you have held on to and the mistaken beliefs that have made you think you are unworthy or unready for love. Or simply visualise yourself leaping into a future free of doubt. Focus on yourself as a being of love, and manifest this into reality by holding on to this deeper truth and reminding yourself often.

Litha : Summer Solstice : Fruition

The summer solstice falls around December 21 or 22 in the southern hemisphere, and June 20 or 21 in the northern hemisphere. It's the longest day and the shortest night of the year, with the sun rising early and setting late (if at all). It marks the peak of energy and solar power of the year before it begins to transition back to the darker half.

Mythologically, this was when the goddess was pregnant with the child she'd conceived with the young god, and bloomed into the mother, filled with new life and potential, while the sun god reached his energetic peak, transforming from young warrior to wise sage.

Astronomically, this solstice occurs when the sun reaches its northern or southernmost latitude. In the southern hemisphere on this day the sun is above the Tropic of Capricorn, and the South Pole is tilted towards the sun at its most extreme angle, making the sun's rays more intense, with more light and heat than at any other time of year. At Midsummer in the northern hemisphere, when the North Pole is tilted towards the sun, it creates the mystical phenomenon known as the Midnight Sun, where in some towns in Norway and Finland the sun doesn't set for up to four months, with a beautiful sun lighting up the sky in the middle of the night – which is balanced out in winter with periods of constant dark known as Polar Night.

The summer solstice, also known as Litha, Alban Heruin (light of the shore), Feast of Epona, Feast of the Fairy, Kupala's Night, Saint John's Day and Mother Night, marks the middle of summer, the famous Midsummer Day and Midsummer Night's Eve so magically captured by Shakespeare. It's the longest day of the year, and is the highest point of the Wheel in terms of heat and light.

In nature it's a time of ripeness and abundance. The grains are growing tall, fruit is swelling with sweetness and colour, animals are out and about, and people feel inspired to stay outdoors, be sociable and celebrate the season of good will and summer fun. Traditionally it was a time of relaxation, as the crops were planted but the harvest was yet to come, so time was taken to rest, restore and enjoy the beautiful weather. Today summer is also a time of holidaying, time off for your own pursuits and basking in the sunshine.

Universally it's a day of high, hot and active energy. Whereas the winter solstice is slow and introspective, its opposite is fast and effective. It's a time to do, to get out there and harness the energising power of the season and make things happen. Follow your passion, take a chance, say yes to new opportunities and express your creativity and your inner self, supported by the vibrant power of this period. This is not the time to be withdrawn or shy, it's for getting out amongst it and making your dreams come true. It's also when relationships –

and you – will mature, and you'll be able to apply new wisdom and experience to your passion, so give thanks for the lessons you have learned and allow the person you are maturing into to unfold.

At the summer solstice everything is ripe and abundant and life is blooming, but there is also the knowledge that, from this day forward, the sun will start to weaken and the days will slowly begin to get shorter as the Wheel of the Year turns back towards winter and the dark half of the year. So this is a day to celebrate, to absorb all the energy of the season and take advantage of every opportunity available, quite literally seizing the day and making hay while the sun shines.

Ways to celebrate

Midsummer has always been a time of festivities, sunshine and joy. Across Asia they had all night parties, feasts and costumed processions in honour of the solar deities, while the Celts and Scandinavians celebrated the longest day by lighting huge bonfires and dancing around them to welcome the sun. These massive fires were lit to bolster the sun's power and ward off evil spirits, ensuring only positive magic entered the human realm. Garlands of flowers were worn to represent the energy of the season, woven with herbs for healing. The summer solstice is the perfect time to harvest your herbs, as they are at their most potent, having absorbed the sun's peaking strength. Saint John's wort, then called chase devil, was picked at this time to repel negativity and bad spirits – and now it is still picked and dried on this day, so it can be used at the winter solstice to combat seasonal affective disorder and recall the energy of the summer.

Today Litha remains a celebration, a day to acknowledge how far you've come and what you've achieved. It's a time to be joyful, wild and free, expressing your inner self and your passion. Enjoy the happiness, energy and abundance of this season, soaking up the sunshine and the festive atmosphere. Spend time at the beach, bathing in the cleansing ocean and frolicking in the sand, or walk through the bush or a park, listening to the lazy buzzing of the bees, the twittering of the birds and the hum of the heat-soaked earth. Make use of the longer days, the enchanted twilight and the extra daylight to have fun, spend time with friends and family or work on your dream.

Long ago, people stayed up throughout Midsummer Night's Eve, around the bonfires or within the sacred circles, then watched the solstice sun rise, feeling it bathe them in warmth and light. If you've got the stamina, echo these ancient rites, performing a vigil through this shortest night. Then, at dawn, stand with your arms outstretched and breathe in the sun's life-giving powers. If you're near a beach or a lake watch it rise over the water, or simply open your bedroom window and let the golden rays of light wash over you with their healing energy and burn away anything you no longer need.

On solstice night, climb a hill and absorb the sun's vitality as it sets in the west, feeling the vibrations of the sunset colours, giving thanks for its warmth and energy, and farewelling it as it begins its descent, and the Wheel starts to turn towards the waning half of the year.

In the southern hemisphere, the summer solstice is when Christmas is celebrated. Rather than the traditional sleet and snow, the sun is strong at this time – some would say merciless – and the energy is fast and active. Despite snow-covered decorations, Santas and hot roast dinners, a legacy of British ancestors, at this time people absorb the solar energy, feast on luscious summer fruits, give thanks for goals reached and blessings received, and revel in the strength and heat of this long day of sunshine and the power of the sun god.

Litha actually sits well with Christmas, being a time of abundance, achievement and culmination, and the sharing of summer's bounty. Organise a festive feast, with everyone bringing food, and wrap pots of sunshiney flowers and summer herbs in gold and red velvet as gifts. Fill a vase with bright summer blooms like daisies, sunflowers, honeysuckle, roses and citrus blossoms to represent the cheeriness of the season, and breathe in their heavenly scent. Plant a sun wheel garden with golden herbs like vervain, Saint John's wort, juniper and rosemary, and bury pieces of citrine and topaz crystals in the earth to encourage abundant growth of the plants as well as your dreams.

This sabbat celebrates the power of the sun to heal and regenerate, and rituals were performed in a range of diverse cultures in honour of sun gods such as Lugh, Apollo and Ra. The Chinese also marked the day with rituals dedicated to Li, the goddess of light, the Japanese worshipped the sun goddess Amaterasu, and in England they honoured Sulis, the Celtic solar deity and patron of the sacred waters at Bath. Invoke the sun god, or simply the masculine aspects of your higher self, along with the sun goddess, or the archetypal energy she embodies, and ask for their blessings for a prosperous and abundant future.

In some communities Midsummer was known as the Feast of the Fairy, when people would leave offerings for the fae folk and petition for their blessings in matters of love and life, so you can also communicate with Maeve or Titania, both queens of the fairies, or any of the other summertime sprites buried deep in your subconscious.

In your journal

This festival of joy and abundance is a great time to take stock of your achievements and acknowledge the progress you've already made and how far you've come. When we strive for something, it's easy to become so focused on the end point that we forget the small victories along the way. To remind me of this, I have a post-it note stuck to my computer saying: "Don't look at how far you have to go, look at how far you've already come." Whenever I feel discouraged, frustrated or stuck, I remind myself of what I have achieved – another hundred books ordered, an article in a British magazine, a great review. My husband likes that quote too, because he sometimes gets so fixated on the progress of his band that he forgets to enjoy what they've already accomplished – the album being released, a video played on national television, a message from a fan in France.

It's important to focus on the big picture, but all the little steps along the way should be sources of immense joy and pride too. Write a list of all the things you've achieved in the last six months, and keep writing, free associating, until you've remembered them all. You could also create a manifestation board to represent your dream, and make an achievement board to hang next to it. Have symbols of what you've already accomplished alongside the things you want to make happen, to add the energy of abundance and success to your hopes. There's nothing like a little victory to keep you motivated!

Use these achievements to inspire you to continue along your path and keep working towards your goals. This solstice is a great time to *do*, to get out there and make things happen, tuning in to the active energy and the heat and vibrant power of the earth. Take action, getting up early or staying up late if need be, and get stuff done.

This is also the perfect time to take note of how your dreams and goals are progressing, and meditate on anything that could be blocking your progress. Be open to letting go of whatever isn't working so you can move forward in the flow that makes progress easier. As you work towards your goal and learn more about the requirements of attaining it, and your own talents and passions, it can be helpful to reassess your methods and work out if you need to head in a new direction. Perhaps you won't need to change a thing, but sometimes there are aspects that can be refined to make your plan more effective.

Creativity and expression are at a peak on this day, so stand in your power and express your needs, saying what you want rather than assuming people know. Misunderstandings can happen easily if you aren't clear and direct in expressing yourself. You do have to work out what your needs and priorities are though before you can express them, so spend time examining your inner world and writing about what you require, personally, professionally and for your own peace of mind. It's not an imposition to express your needs, it's a right.

You can also use the heat and energy of summer to purify and burn away anything that no longer serves you. In times gone by people would use the summer bonfires for a ritual of releasement, throwing a symbol of what they wanted to put behind them into the flames. You can use a red or orange candle or a tiny cauldron to burn yours away, or simply stand outside in the sunshine and let it cleanse you of doubt and fear so you can step forward into your future with dazzling confidence and vibrant summery energy.

Lughnasadh: First Day of Autumn: Gratitude

Lughnasadh, the cross-quarter day which marks the beginning of autumn, falls in the first week of February in the southern hemisphere, and the first week of August in the northern hemisphere. It's the first harvest festival, a time of feasting, celebration and thanksgiving for the life-giving properties of the grain.

Mythologically, this was the time of the waning god, as the solar deity who had peaked at the summer solstice began to lose his power and strength. In some traditions he was cut down by the goddess, along with the harvest, in order to fertilise the land and ensure abundance for the coming year. He was the sacrificial god, a theme echoed in religions around the world, tied to the forces of nature and the cycle of death and rebirth. And the goddess was the bountiful mother as well as the wielder of the scythe, and continued her pregnancy alone, knowing her companion would be reborn at Yule.

Astronomically, this cross-quarter day falls midway between the summer solstice and the autumn equinox. In the southern hemisphere, it occurs when the sun is halfway between the Tropic of Capricorn and the Equator, on its way back north, in the same position as it was at Beltane as it headed south towards summer.

Lughnasadh, also known as Lammas, First Harvest, Bread Harvest, Tailtiu's Feast and Festival of First Fruits, signifies the end of summer and the first day of autumn. The earth still throbs with life and energy, but it's mature, fully ripened, almost over-abundant energy. It's often still hot at this time of year, especially in Australia, but the strength of the sun is beginning to wane, and cooling breezes and crisp air start to temper the warmth of the days, particularly in the enchanted twilight hours. The trees begin to turn red-gold-orange-rust, the night comes a little earlier, and the first crops are ready to harvest.

Another name for this festival is Lammas, from the Old English hlaf, meaning loaf, and maesse, meaning feast, because traditionally it was on this day that the first loaf of bread was baked from the first harvest. In medieval England this was transformed into a Christian festival of thanksgiving, although it was still steeped in pagan traditions such as sharing nature's bounty with the poor and sacrificing the first fruits in honour of the god or goddess, adding to the sacrificial symbolism of this festival. As the first harvest was brought in, people took a few days off to rest, relax and celebrate, and honour the earth mother for the food that would keep them going through the winter months. Soldiers would return from war to help bring in the harvest, so it was also a time of reunions with family and loved ones.

While Litha was a celebration of the strength of the god, Lughnasadh honoured the goddess and her abundance, represented by the grains that kept people alive. Along with bread, corn dollies were made from the husks of the first cereals to be harvested, symbolising the deification of the crops and the importance of the harvest. These "dollies" were an embodiment of the goddess, and were kept in the home until spring, when they were ploughed back into the earth with the first seeds to increase fertility, thus continuing the cycle of life, death and rebirth.

Ways to celebrate

The beginning of autumn has long been a time of thanksgiving and revelry in appreciation of nature's bounty. In Ancient Rome they honoured Saturn, the god of agriculture and the harvest, while in Greece it was Demeter, the goddess of the grain. In Ghana in West Africa they celebrate the harvest festival of Homowo, which means hooting at hunger. It commemorates a devastating famine and the agricultural methods they developed to prevent future ones, and is celebrated with feasting, music and ritual. In China during Chung Yuan, the Hungry Ghost Festival, food is left out to appease the spirits who return at this time, while in the Aztec lands the harvest festival of Tlacaxipehualiztli honoured Xipe Totec, god of vegetation and renewal.

Across the British Isles this first harvest festival was celebrated with feasting, craft fairs, horse markets, games and contests, many in honour of Lugh, the Celtic sun god. Handfastings also took place at these fairs, with people being bound in marriage for a year and a day, and wooden cart wheels were dipped in tar then set alight and ceremonially rolled down a hill to signify the waning of the sun's – and the sun god's – power as summer came to an end. He was seen as a sacrifice, going down into the underworld until his resurrection.

In his honour people sacrificed the first sheaf of corn, the first wheat stalk, the first fruits, the first loaf of bread, back to the land and to the earth mother. A libation of mead and an offering of food was part of all their rituals, but at this time of year it became a major part of the proceedings. There are even legends of human sacrifice and death, of kings offering their life in order to return power to the land as it began to waste away and enter the fallow winter period.

Today, the beginning of autumn is still a time of first harvests. Fruit picking is a popular job for many travellers, with farms all over the country taking on seasonal workers. The grape harvesting and wine making begins, and golden wheat fields cover the paddocks. You can create your own little ceremony by going to a farm and enjoying the first fruits of the season fresh from the vine, absorbing the energy of the earth and the life force that flows through the planet.

But this festival is also about harvesting the fruits of your labours, and acknowledging your successes and what you've achieved in the past year. It's a time to celebrate the goals you've reached and have your own festival of gratitude, in whatever form that takes. Toast your success, throw a party, reward yourself for your hard work with a gift you've long wanted, some time off to rest and chill out, or even a trip away to mark the occasion. Invite your friends over and bake bread or muffins, infusing them with gratitude for the plentiful food we enjoy, and feast on fresh organic produce.

Then, out of gratitude and in the spirit of the ancestors who shared the bounty of their harvest with those less well off, pass on some of your good fortune. Make a donation to a local charity, support World Vision or another group giving aid to feed people in impoverished nations, lend money to women setting up a business in the developing world through Kiva.org or give some time to help a friend or family member, ensuring the energy of abundance continues and is strengthened. Give out of grace and for joy, without any expectation of receiving anything in return. Such small sacrifices reflect the essence of Lughnasadh, and help create future abundance and prosperity.

Long ago, people used this time to prepare for the coming winter by storing food, making jams, sorting out their possessions, fixing leaking roofs and mending tools and fences. You can also plan ahead, setting things in motion now that will pay off later. Learn a skill you might need, research the next step in your project, or work on letting go of a fear that has been holding you back. Even as the harvest is brought in, the seeds to be sown next year are gathered and stored, in a continual dance of planting, growing and culmination.

In your journal

As well as a time of feasting and thanksgiving for the harvesting of the crops, and recognition of the eternal cycle of sowing and reaping, Lughnasadh is also about the symbolic things you grow and create in your life. It's a day to harvest what you planted earlier in the year and celebrate your successes. Make a list of all the things you've gained – the goals you reached, the gifts you've been given, the new talents you've developed, the friends you've made, the experiences you've had, the healings you've received, the opportunities you've pursued – and how you have developed and changed as a result of them.

Create a ritual of appreciation that is meaningful for you. You may want to journal about it, exploring in depth the things you've learned and the ways in which you've grown, send thank you cards to people who have helped you work towards your goals, start a gratitude diary or write a poem that outlines all that you're grateful for. We may no longer be so connected to the production of our food, as in days gone by, or believe that our prayers or sacrifices influence the success of a crop, but appreciating what we have and giving thanks for it is still a beautiful way to live, and can increase our own attitude of abundance.

Also acknowledge all the things you've achieved so you can share your successes with others. Don't be modest or downplay how far you've come, because you'll inspire other people with stories of your breakthroughs, your dedication and details of how you overcame the obstacles you faced. Your successes will help them realise they can also pursue their dreams, and will hopefully give them the motivation they need to get started on their own journey.

Don't ever diminish yourself or your achievements, or let anyone else do so. Be proud of your light, your talents and all your accomplishments, and always allow yourself to shine brightly and illuminate the darkness for others. As American author Marianne Williamson says: "Your playing small doesn't serve the world. There's nothing enlightened about shrinking so that other people won't feel insecure around you. We are all meant to shine, and as we let our own light shine, we give other people permission to do the same."

Around Lughnasadh, as the energy begins to subtly slow and the tides of the earth start to ebb, it's also a time to be patient and to trust that everything is as it should be, because there are still harvests to come. Not everything has to be achieved right now – some things take longer to manifest. The lesson of the Wheel of the Year is that everything continues, everything happens when it should and everything is eternal. This can be hard to accept when you're desperate to fulfil a dream (believe me, I know, I'm totally impatient!), but often waiting for more information, or taking the time to plan fully rather than rushing into a project and starting before you have everything you need, is more efficient in the long run and will help you reach your goal quicker.

Also consider whether there are any things you regret. Did you aim for something that didn't pan out, or become involved in a painful situation? Write about them, pouring out your heart, and your pain, your regrets and your bitterness. Then let them go. Regret and bitterness are the most destructive of emotions, and they'll hold you back and poison all your good intentions.

If you want to do a ritual, pour all of your troubles into a stone, a piece of paper, a corn husk or a pine cone, either by holding the object and using the power of intention to transfer your emotions into it, employing a shamanic technique to physically blow your pain into it, or sleeping with it under your pillow so it can absorb everything you want to let go of. Then throw it into a river or a fire, and feel yourself lightening up as you release the burdens you've held on to.

Lughnasadh is the festival of symbolic harvesting, contemplation and emotional cleansing. At the cross-quarter days the veil between the worlds is considered to be thinner than at other times, and at this one you can connect with your own higher self and do inner work. Let go of the things that are holding you back so you can lay the foundation for future harvests and move forward into the light.

Mabon : Autumn Equinox : Harvest

The autumn equinox falls around March 20 or 21 in the southern hemisphere and September 22 or 23 in the northern hemisphere. It's characterised by the length of day and night being equal as the sun travels across the Equator to the other hemisphere, and is the moment of balance in nature and within – a time of harmony, joy and calm.

Mythologically, this was when the god had aged and was declining in power, becoming a shadow deity as he prepared to leave the earth to descend to the underworld. The goddess was also ageing, absorbing the energy of the crone and wise woman. She was saddened by the impending "death" of the god, yet comforted that life was growing within her. This was also when the harvest deity Demeter had to farewell her daughter Persephone, who spent six months of each year in the underworld as the bride of Hades. She returned to him at the autumn equinox, which explained why the nights started to grow longer than the days from this point onwards – the grieving Demeter made the earth barren until her daughter's return in the spring.

Astronomically, this is one of only two times that the length of day and night is the same, as the sun sits directly above the Equator, creating 12 hours of light and 12 hours of dark in each hemisphere. The autumn equinox represents the triumph of the dark over the light, because for the next six months, until the spring equinox, the nights will become longer than the days and the weather will get cooler.

The autumn equinox, also known as Mabon, Alban Elued (light of the water), Harvest Home, Feast of Avalon, Festival of the Vine and Cornucopia, marks the middle of autumn. It's a time of crisp, chilly mornings, pale skies and a world aflame with colour as the trees turn a hundred shades of red-orange-yellow-gold-brown. Daylight savings ends, the weather turns cool and things in nature slow down, turn inward and begin to wither. The leaves start to fall – hence the American reference to the season as "fall" – and farmers commence the second harvest, also known as the green or wild harvest, when fruits, vegetables and remaining crops are brought in from the fields.

Vibrationally it's a season of withdrawal, of being alone to meditate, recharge, reassess and ponder where you're at in life. The energy of the earth retreats and goes within, as does your personal power, but from this experience you'll emerge with immense strength and new wisdom.

This is the time of balance – the world is poised between summer and winter and day and night are equal, which is reflected in each of us. You can ensure personal balance by acknowledging and integrating all the parts of your self and beginning to look within, echoing the path of the god, who prepares to sacrifice himself and descend to the underworld where the Mysteries will unfold. Acknowledge the things you've sacrificed, and others have sacrificed for you, to be where you are now. Give thanks for your metaphorical harvest, honouring your achievements, experiences and wisdom in a way that feels right to you, be it with a big celebration or a personal ritual of gratitude.

Ways to celebrate

As the second harvest festival, Mabon continues the theme of thanksgiving for the bounty of nature that began at Lughnasadh. In the Celtic lands, Mid-Autumn was a time of celebration and rituals to give thanks for a successful crop and honour the abundance of the village. Offerings were made to the gods to implore them to provide enough food so people could survive through the winter, and feasts were held to reinforce the magic and energy of the harvest.

Corn dollies were made from the last sheaf of the crop being harvested – wheat, oats, corn, rye or barley, depending on the area – and kept inside throughout the winter to house the spirit of the grain, which they believed became homeless after the harvest, when the crops were cut down. When seeds were sown in spring these decorated stalks were returned to the earth, ploughed into the newly prepared fields to imbue them with the energy and intent of the goddess and begin the cycle of growth and rebirth again. Churches in England have also marked this day since the 1800s, when they started decorating the church with fresh local produce, singing hymns of thanksgiving, and bringing in food to be distributed to the poor.

To celebrate the season, prepare a harvest feast for friends, with earth-coloured fruits and vegetables, spices, nuts, pumpkin pie, golden grains and heavy warm breads. Decorate the table with autumn leaves, wildflowers, acorns, dried ears of corn and herbs. Wear a garland of ivy, and orange, yellow or brown clothes, and tie golden ribbons in your hair. Donate food or money to a charity that feeds the homeless or the poor in recognition that today, as in times gone by, there are still many people who struggle to survive the winter months.

In Japan, Buddhists celebrate the autumn equinox, and the three days before and after it, with a festival called Higan. Traditionally it acknowledged that the harvest was in and people had more time to contemplate their spiritual beliefs and rededicate themselves to their path. Today the week-long period also commemorates the ancestors, and is marked by cemetery visits, offerings of flowers and food, and the burning of incense to take their prayers to the heavens.

In China, the harvest celebration is known as the Mid-Autumn or Mooncake Festival, and takes place at the harvest moon, the full moon closest to the autumn equinox. Lanterns are made and floated down rivers, and there is feasting, fire-dragon dancing, music, family reunions and the baking and eating of mooncakes. These delicacies consist of a thin pastry layer surrounding a sweeter filling inside, and often have an egg yolk cooked within to represent the harvest moon. They are embossed with Chinese characters for longevity or harmony, or decorated with pictures of the moon and other harvest images.

The Mid-Autumn Festival celebrates the harvest, and the abundance nature offers up at this time. Apples, grapes, pomegranates and other foods are placed on altars as offerings to the harvest gods and the moon goddess, and family dinners are held, with people travelling across the country to attend this thanksgiving ritual. The harvest moon appears to be the fullest, brightest, biggest and most golden of the year. It was vital to farmers, who had to work all night to get the harvest in, as it allowed them to see by its golden light.

Another way to absorb the energy of this day of balance is to take up yoga, which will harmonise and balance you physically, emotionally, mentally and spiritually. Becoming strong in body also strengthens your mind and helps you cope with emotional storms in a calmer manner, as well as boosting your confidence and inner strength.

In your journal

Mabon is a harvest festival, so it's a time to honour and celebrate your achievements and feel fulfilment and pride from each one. Write about the things you've manifested in the six weeks since Lughnasadh, and any goals you've reached or lessons you've learned. This is also a powerful time to release what no longer serves you in order to move forward. In the wild, old growth is cleared. In your life, cut out anything that's holding you back, draining you or preventing new life and love from flourishing, whether it's work, a person, a belief system, a regret or an echo from the past. Many plants grow better, and produce more abundantly, if they are pruned regularly; likewise you will have more energy and time, and be more productive, if you let go of the things or situations that are dragging you down emotionally and wearing you out. Sometimes this is as simple as saying no to requests that leave you no time for your own needs, but you may have to go deep to discover what you would benefit from cutting out of your life.

You can do an exercise to connect to the energy of Persephone, visualising yourself descending down into an underworld cavern and exploring the darkness of your psyche and unearthing the answers that are hidden within your subconscious. If it's easier, picture yourself communicating with the goddess, and write down everything she says to you. Otherwise, converse with your higher self and open up to the wisdom you already hold within. Some people use this ritual to unravel mother-daughter issues, since Persephone and her mother Demeter were so entwined, but it is also effective for uncovering any hidden concerns and finding answers to the secret yearnings of your heart.

The equinox is also about balance, and ensuring harmony in your life by maintaining your emotional and physical health, and integrating all the parts of your deeper self. Consider whether you're spending enough time relaxing, expressing your spirituality, being with friends and on your own. Are you getting enough sleep, exercise, nutrition or down time? Your physical wellbeing is crucial to your emotional and spiritual health, which in turn affects your vitality and energy levels. It's all about balance, and while the energies of the earth are in alignment, it's a good time to weigh up how balanced you are, and take steps to even the scales if you're out of whack in any area.

It's also a powerful time to heal rifts, resolve arguments and seek harmony in your life. Whether the other person is ready to work on the issue isn't important – finding resolution and forgiving those involved, including yourself, within your own heart can bring immense personal healing, make you feel lighter, happier and stronger and help you move forward with grace and wisdom.

It's a good time to explore your shadow side too, and bring any perceived darkness out into the light to be balanced and illuminated. Suppressing anger or stewing on a problem can blow it out of proportion, so journal about your issues or fears to release the intensity and allow space for lightness and resolution to emerge. Acknowledge and respect your so-called negative emotions, for you have a right to them, and as long as you don't drown or wallow in them, they can be a powerful catalyst for change. Experiencing and expressing anger doesn't make you a bad person. Life is all about balance – being a healer and nurturer when needed, but allowing yourself to go into battle and fight injustice when necessary. Expressing anger constructively is far better, and healthier, than suppressing it, and finding your own power is about embracing every part of yourself – the light and the dark, the healer and the warrior, the sweet and the strong.

As the shadows lengthen, it's also a good time to scry if you want insight into your future. If you can, light a fire and stare into the flames, allowing your mind to go blank and your vision to blur a little. Note any images you see. Or go outside and watch the clouds scuttling across the sky and analyse the shapes you see within them. Without thinking about it too much, write down what they mean to you.

Pyromancy (fire reading) and nephomancy (cloud reading) are forms of divination that have been used for millennia. You should develop your own dictionary of symbols through regular practise, because you know better than anyone else what each symbol means to you, but you can begin with standard readings, such as a heart indicating new romance, a cat referring to the need to trust your intuition, a tree meaning you'll make new friends and a plane foreshadowing travel. You can also use oracle cards or any other form of divination, tapping in to your intuitive powers in the most effective way you know how, and letting the truths of your heart and soul reveal themselves to you.

Samhain: First Day of Winter: Death

Samhain, the festival of the ancestors and the dead that marks the beginning of winter, falls in early May in the southern hemisphere and early November in the northern hemisphere – and on October 31 in popular culture, where it is celebrated as Halloween. It honours the Wheel of the Year as it turns towards the barrenness of winter, in nature and in our lives, and is a time of withdrawal and withering.

Mythologically, this was when the goddess became the crone, the old one, the wise one – the earth mother who understood, and taught others, that we need darkness and death to have light and rebirth. In some traditions the god descended to the underworld on this day, to await his transformation at the winter solstice; in others he was already there and the goddess returned to be reunited with her consort.

Astronomically, this cross-quarter day falls midway between the autumn equinox and the winter solstice. In the southern hemisphere, it's when the sun is halfway between the Equator and the Tropic of Cancer, on its way north for winter, and it rises in the same position as it will at Imbolc. In the northern hemisphere Samhain occurs six months later, when the sun is heading south from the Equator down to the Tropic of Capricorn.

Samhain, also known as Halloween, All Souls Eve, Day of the Dead, Feast of Spirits, Shadow Fest and Ancestor Night, marks the end of autumn and the start of the coldness and dark of winter. The crispness and vivid flame-coloured beauty of autumn fades as the energy of the earth withdraws and nature starts to wither and die. Animals begin to migrate or hibernate, and while the grass may become green and lush with the onset of rain, many of the trees are stripped bare, with bitterly cold winds adding to the starkness of the season.

This was the third and last harvest of the year, when anything left in the fields, from wheat and oats to turnips and apples, would be gathered in and stored for the barren months ahead. Snow covered the land and fresh food was scarce. Cattle and sheep were brought in from the summer paddocks to the barns, and those who couldn't find food or shelter were slaughtered and preserved for later eating. Wood was chopped and peat stacked for the winter fires, herbs were dried and food was baked and preserved. Families gathered together to prepare and ready themselves for winter, and there was an air of celebration and abundance even as the hard months approached.

Symbolically the energy is also about preparing for what's ahead, harvesting and releasing the things you've been holding on to and readying yourself for new challenges and experiences. Winter is a season of introspection and darkness, both metaphorically and literally, which encourages you to slow down and withdraw a little to conserve mental energy. It's a time for inner reflection and contemplation, of studying the Mysteries – of your magical tradition or your life – and scrying for answers and illumination. At each of the four cross-quarter days the veil between the worlds was considered to be thinner than usual, and at this one people connected with the energy of the ancestors, the spirits and the dead, calling on them for wisdom and knowledge about the future as well as the past.

Samhain was the Celtic New Year, the most important, sacred and magical celebration of the pagan calendar. Rituals were performed, elaborate feasts were held, and hearth fires were extinguished in every home so they could be relit from a special druidic fire in each community, which brought blessings and new light to the coming year, and rekindled the hopes and dreams that had been slumbering.

Ways to celebrate

Samhain is a festival of the dead, but it's not scary or gloomy – rather it's a celebration and honouring of those who have passed, and of the memories of all the beautiful times you had with them. It was believed that on this day the ghosts, the gods and the spirits came close to the earth and walked amongst humans, visiting their old homes and checking in with their families, so offerings were made to them in the hope that they would impart their wisdom and reveal the future. Some people set an extra place at the dinner table for their loved ones who had passed over, while others cast spells to bring their spirit back to the land of the living or did mediumship rituals to try to converse.

In Latin America this celebration is known as the Day of the Dead, el Dia de los Muertos, a four-thousand-year-old ritual where families and friends gather together to pray for, honour and remember those who have died. Catholic traditions have melded into the proceedings, but originally the festival was dedicated to the Aztec goddess Mictecacihuatl, the queen of the underworld who guards the bones of the dead. It's marked with festivals, parades and visits to cemeteries with offering of flowers, food and other gifts. Candy or chocolate skulls are exchanged to represent the theme of life, death and rebirth so intrinsic to this day, and people communicate with those who have died, petitioning them with prayers as the Celts did at Samhain.

This magical time and its purpose has been conserved in the modern-day festival of Halloween, which celebrates ghosts, witches, bats and magic, and the Christian holidays of All Hallows Eve and All Saints Day. The Christian version echoes the old pagan meaning, with prayers being offered for the souls of those who have crossed over.

To absorb the energy of Samhain, prepare a harvest feast, with pumpkins, winter vegetables, nuts, grains, apple pies, cider and spiced wine. Decorate the table with orange and black, dress up in magical costumes and, as night falls, light black candles to illuminate the room and emphasise the deepening shadows. Lay out a plate for your lost loved ones and share your favourite recollections of them, balancing the sombreness of the occasion with happy, funny stories.

After feasting, or instead of if you'd rather celebrate alone, do some divination. Bob for apples, divine the future with nuts or try other psychic games involving the fruits of the harvest. Apples are considered very sacred, and are associated with the fairies and with magic and transformation. Legends tell of enchanted apples with the power of immortality, cutting one in half crossways reveals a five-pointed star, symbol of the goddess, and they were involved in divination rituals such as peeling one to discover the initial of your future love.

As well as remembering those who have passed, it's also important to honour those who are still here, so it's the perfect time to call your parents, visit your grandparents or write to someone who meant a lot to you when you were growing up, and thank them for the moments they shared with you and the influence they had on your life. Too often we don't recognise someone's worth until they've passed away, so make sure you celebrate your loved ones while they're with you, and let the people in your life know how you feel about them. When a friend of mine took his own life, the biggest regret his mates had was that they hadn't expressed how much they cared about him and how important he was to them while they had the chance.

Samhain is a fire festival, so the element of fire is a big part of it. In ages past, bonfires lit up the long night to ward off evil spirits, purify the land and its people, and bring hope and illumination to the darkness. Today this still goes on across the British Isles, although many of the fires are now lit in the name of Guy Fawkes, which has a different meaning yet still echoes the ancient purpose of farewelling the summer and welcoming the stark, powerful beauty of winter. If you can't have an outdoor fire, light a small one in your cauldron, or just ignite a black candle, and watch the light chase the shadows away. Toss a symbol of the dying year into the flames so you can start the new one with a fresh slate, or visualise the cleansing of any regrets that are weighing you down.

In the southern hemisphere it can be hard to explain to people that you're celebrating "Halloween" in May, but if you pay attention to the earth, to nature and to the seasons, it's clear that this is the time of Samhain and its energy of introspection, transformation and release.

In your journal

If you've lost someone close to you, light a candle for them and revel in all your memories. Look at photos or letters they sent and feel their presence with you. If you believe in an after-life, try to communicate with them, using automatic writing or scrying, or just write your favourite recollections of them in your journal. Look out for signs that they could be near – a whiff of their perfume, their favourite song on the radio, a flash of them out of the corner of your eye. This festival shouldn't be morbid – it's about celebrating their life and all that they meant to you, and remembering their impact on your heart.

The energy of Samhain inspires a mood of self-examination and contemplation, so reflect on those you've lost to distance or estrangement, and acknowledge anything that has come to an end in your life. You don't have to fix the problem or make up with people if a relationship has run its course, but honour the good times and the lessons learned, and perform a farewell ritual to release any residual pain and attachment. If you've had a painful break up, go through your home and find any reminders of the person, be it photos, their clothes or gifts they gave you, and get rid of them. It doesn't matter whether you throw them out, post them back, give them to charity or burn them, just let them go so you can start to heal.

As the end of one year and the beginning of the next, this is the perfect time to let go of the energy of the past and of old memories so you can move forward with lightness and strength. Light a black candle and, by its flickering illumination, write out all the worries, frustrations, regrets and seeming failures you've held on to over the past 12 months. Visualise the fire of the candle flame burning them away and leaving you purified and refreshed, and breathe in this positive new energy. Then burn the list in the flame, releasing your attachment to those emotions and their power over you.

Also work out which habits and traits you want to bring into the new year, and which you want to leave behind. Examine any negative patterns or behaviours you want to release, or anything you're scared of or dreading. Samhain is a powerful time for banishing rituals and releasement ceremonies, as they are supported by the energy of the season, so face your fears and relinquish your baggage to the light.

On this mystical, mysterious night, when the Otherworld reaches out and imprints upon ours, tap in to your own crone energy and find the wisdom within to examine your life and your progress. Take a long hard look at where you're at and what you're doing, and your actions, motives and beliefs. Consider whether you're truly following your heart, or if you feel you've wasted time this year, pursuing things you don't really care about, treating your body with less respect than it deserves, being too nice at the expense of your needs. Stand in your power and connect with your inner self and core beliefs, delving deep into your psyche to learn how to be true to yourself and your life path.

This energetic new year is a gateway, a threshold you can cross to move into a new way of being. It can be hard work at times, filled with sometimes painful self-examination and remembering, but out of this darkness comes regeneration, renewal and transformation, and a new sense of personal power and magic.

The Phases of the Moon

The moon, the biggest, brightest, most beautiful object in the night sky, is a thing of mystery, enchantment and wonder, linked to intuition, inner power and imagination. To the Celts, its phases reflected the phases of a human life – birth, adolescence, adulthood, death and rebirth – and were associated with the Triple Goddess who included the aspects of maiden, mother and crone, represented by Rhiannon, maiden goddess of inspiration and the waxing moon, Arianrhod, mother goddess of fertility and the full moon, and Ceridwen, crone goddess of death, rebirth and the waning moon. In countless other cultures the moon was also seen as a goddess, who not only marked the passing of time, but increased fertility, deepened psychic powers and improved wellbeing.

Harnessing the energy of the phases of the moon can add magic to your life and help bring a goal to fruition. These phases are determined by the moon's position in relation to the earth and the sun, as it orbits our planet every 29.5 days. The moon has no light of its own – it's illuminated by the light of the sun reflecting off its surface, and its phases are created by the amount of the illuminated side we can see.

You can picture these phases by imagining a clock. The earth sits in the centre of the clock face, with the sun above 12 o'clock. The moon is at the end of the minute hand, circling around the clock face – and the earth – in an anticlockwise direction. It begins its cycle at 12, directly between the sun and the earth, which makes the moon invisible to us because the side that's reflecting the light of the sun is facing away from the earth, towards the sun. This is the dark moon.

A day or two later, as the moon moves towards 11 o'clock, a tiny sliver of the illuminated side can be seen, which appears as a thin crescent. This is the new moon. In the southern hemisphere it looks like a C, while in the northern hemisphere it's reversed, appearing as a backward C, and at the equator it's horizontal rather than vertical.

The crescent continues to increase as the moon moves from between the earth and the sun, and the angle between them allows us to see more of the moon's reflected light. By the time it gets to nine o'clock, which takes about a week, it's at right angles to the earth in relation to the sun, and we see a half circle. This is the first quarter moon.

When the moon gets to six o'clock, it's on the other side of the earth from the sun, with the earth in between. The whole of the side that is visible to us is reflecting back sunlight, so we see a round moon in all its shining, golden glory. This is the full moon. The size of the moon hasn't changed, it's just that we're seeing the fully illuminated side.

After that it appears to decrease as it progresses back to the dark moon. When it gets to three o'clock we again see a half moon, but this time it's facing the other direction, a C in the north and a reverse C in the south. This is the third or last quarter moon. From there it continues back to 12, with the crescent getting smaller each night, until it returns to the beginning, where it's invisible again, and the cycle starts over.

Lunar phases are printed in newspapers, moon diaries and websites like www.sunrisesunset.com, and you can also determine the phase of the moon by its shape, as well as the time it rises, which occurs about 50 minutes later each day. It can be remembered by the old adage: "The new moon rises at sunrise, and the first quarter at noon. The full moon rises at sunset, and the last quarter at midnight."

As the moon goes from dark to full it's the waxing or growing period, a time of new beginnings, growing vitality and increasing energy. As it goes from full back to dark it's the waning period, a time of lowering energy and introspection. Magical practitioners use the cycles of the moon to increase the power of spellworking, harnessing the universal energies inherent in each phase. So do fishermen, who understand the incredible pull the moon has on the tides of the ocean and its creatures.

Gardening also operates to the rhythms of the moon, as its phase can enhance or hinder plant growth. To boost it, sow crops that produce above the ground in the period between new moon and full, as the light and energy increases, and crops that produce below ground, such as root vegetables and bulbs, between full moon and dark.

Surfers understand its power too. The full moon magnifies weather patterns, so a winter moon will bring stormier swells and bigger waves. The tides are more extreme at both the full moon and the dark moon – high tides are higher, and low tides lower. These two phases have an intense influence on the ocean, heightening conditions and drawing huge swells – or, if the ocean is flat, making it even flatter. Surfers going to Indonesia for a wave-riding safari book around a full moon, so they'll have optimum conditions and even bigger waves.

Hair growth is also influenced by the moon. If you want your hair to grow faster, trim the ends between the new moon and the first quarter. If you want it to grow thicker and fuller, trim it during the full moon phase. And if you really like the style and want to maintain it, have it cut around the third quarter, so it grows out more slowly.

The moon affects tides, plants, animals and the behaviour of people. Some can't sleep during the full moon, others feel more emotional or have strange dreams. It's common to feel more energetic during the waxing phase, and more tired when it's waning. There are also many tales of accidents and psychic breakdown increasing at the full moon. Today the moon's journey across the sky is obscured by buildings, and even women's cycles, which used to be intimately connected to the moon, are now controlled by chemicals. But it still affects our energy and emotions, and can be used to influence the outcome and power of rituals and spells, and empower any project you want to complete.

Moon Magic

One lunar cycle runs for 29.5 days, beginning with the tiny crescent of the new moon, building in energy through the waxing phase to the full moon, then decreasing and withdrawing through the waning period to the dark moon, before starting a new cycle. Here's how to take advantage of the phases of the moon to set your goal or intention and watch it grow to beautiful, abundant completion.

New Moon: Day 1

The new moon rises just after dawn and remains up all day, often unnoticed in contrast to the bright sky, and sets just after sunset. From the moment the tiny new crescent moon is first sighted, and for a day or two afterwards, is a time of heightened energy and new beginnings. It's a good time to start new projects, make resolutions and vows you want to stick to, go in a new direction, invite something new into your life or look for a different job. Chinese New Year always falls on a new moon, as it brings energy and vitality to the coming year.

This is the time to plant seeds, both literally and metaphorically, be it in the garden or in your life, sowing the seeds of new ideas, dreams and hopes. Magical workings are most powerful during the day, when the moon is visible; during this phase there is no moon at night.

A simple yet powerful new moon ritual is to sit outside as dawn breaks, watching the sun rise and feeling the energy of the new moon as it peeks above the horizon, and write down your wish for the coming month. Work out an affirmation to support it, and keep it somewhere you'll see it often as you harness the power of this lunar cycle to make it come true. The new moon's power is embryonic – if you plant a seed now, its power will continue to grow as the moon does. You can also invoke maiden moon goddesses such as Rhiannon, Bridie, Persephone and Maia to add sweet, innocent yet powerful energy to your intent.

Waxing Moon: Days 1 to 14

During the two weeks from new moon to full, the energy is strong and positive, so concentrate on attracting and drawing things to you. It's the optimal time for magical workings to manifest love, abundance and new career opportunities, and for learning new things, expanding your outlook, increasing spirituality and boosting fertility. In the waxing period the lunar energy continues to build, so whatever seeds you planted at the new moon will sprout rapidly. It's an energy of gathering, growing, strengthening and increase, so if you need to release something while the moon is waxing, reverse the intent of the spell so it fits with the energies. Rather than giving up smoking by releasing your addiction, create a ceremony to attract willpower to you.

If you're doing healings, draw good health to you when the moon is waxing, and release illness when it's waning. Maiden goddesses can also be invoked, such as Bridie, Artemis, Athena, Aphrodite and Aine.

Waxing crescent moon: Days 1 to 6

In the week following the new moon, it rises a little later each day, through the morning, and sets after sunset. This is the sprouting phase, when you nurture the seeds you planted at the new moon. It's the time to set things in motion, and brings energy and new growth to projects, helping you manifest them into reality and flooding you with strength and the energy of growth. The sliver of light represents your growing consciousness and the dawning of your potential.

Waxing half moon – the first quarter: Days 7 to 8

At the end of the first week is the first quarter moon, which rises at noon and sets at midnight (this is why you can see it in the evening but not in the morning, as it's on the other side of the world then). It's halfway between new and full, and looks like a half moon. This is the growth phase, where you build upon what you've already begun, although the energy can be challenging at times, pushing you towards achieving your goals and urging you to work hard to get projects done. Issues can come to a head, which is all part of the process of growth.

Waxing gibbous moon: Days 9 to 14

In the second week of the lunar cycle, as the moon moves towards full, it rises in the afternoon and sets in the early hours of the morning. This phase is conducive to expressing yourself, getting in touch with your feelings and taking action. It requires some patience, as things are almost, but not quite, at the peak of their potential and energy.

Full Moon: Days 14 to 16

The full moon rises as the sun sets, which is why it's so obvious and clearly seen, because it sails across the sky all night, contrasting with the velvety blackness, before setting around dawn, just as the sun is rising. The three days of the full moon – the day of, the day before and the day after – can be used to boost any intention or project. It represents achievement, culmination and abundance. The world is filled with energy and potential, so it's a great time for healing and manifestation.

Midnight is the most powerful time for magical work, as the moon is directly overhead. Stand beneath the golden orb and give thanks for what you've achieved so far, and breathe in the energy and power so you can harness it for self-expression and inner strength. Perform a Drawing Down the Moon ritual, bringing the energy of the moon, and the moon goddess, into your heart and soul. This is a great time to charge crystals and amulets with the moon's energy, and cleanse your own physical and etheric bodies. Psychic abilities are also at their strongest, so practise any divination methods you are drawn to, looking within to find answers to your questions and clues to your future.

The full moon is the high tide of power in a lunar cycle, so cast spells for completion, things you want to achieve, and anything requiring an extra boost of intensity, such as healing work, job hunting or love. You can also invoke the mother goddesses Arianrhod, Isis, Selene, Diana, Lakshmi, Quan Yin, Demeter, Ishtar and Mama Quilla, who all represent the full moon, motherhood, fertility, the earth and creation.

Waning Moon: Days 16 to 29

During the two weeks from full moon to dark, the energy is slowing down, so it's a time for banishing and release work. Do a ritual to let go of anything that no longer serves you, such as a past relationship, a bad habit, a trait like procrastination, or any material objects or issues weighing you down and blocking your progress. If you need to attract something while the moon is waning, reverse the intent. Rather than doing a spell to draw new love to you, which works against the energy of this phase, cast one to banish loneliness. This is a time of retreat and withdrawal, when you can invoke darker crone energy goddesses such as Ceridwen, the Morrigan and Grandmother Spiderwoman, who hold the wisdom and power of transformation, endings and rebirth.

Waning gibbous moon: Days 16 to 21

In the week following the full moon, it rises a little later each day, between dusk and midnight, and sets in the morning. This is a phase of introspection and self-assessment. In the garden this energy promotes root development; in life it's a time to stand strong and find your inner power, delving within for the answers imparted by the full moon. Magical workings are most effective from midnight to dawn, particularly releasement rituals to banish things, people or situations from your life.

Waning half moon – third quarter: Days 22 to 23

At the end of the third week is the third quarter moon, which rises around midnight and sets at midday, so if you see a half moon in the morning it's this waning one, but if you see it in the afternoon it's the waxing first quarter. It brings a reflective energy, and is the time to assimilate what you've learned, achieved and still need to do. If an issue requires resolution, work your magic and put your intent out to the universe. The energy is waning, but you can draw it inside for later use. Work on banishing illness, addictions, negativity and bad habits – anything that will slow the fruition of your earlier spellworking.

Waning crescent moon: Days 24 to 29

In the fourth week, as the moon moves towards dark, it rises in the early hours of the morning and sets in the afternoon. This is the letting go phase, a time to release and banish anything you don't need so you can prepare again for the fresh beginnings of the new moon. It's the closing of the cycle, the time to reap what you sowed at the start of the month and integrate the lessons you've learned. You've done the inner work, and now you must release the outcome to the universe.

Dark Moon: Day 29

The dark moon rises at dawn, with the sun, and sets at sunset. It is between the earth and the sun the whole time, making it invisible to us. While some people take the dark moon as a day off from magic, others use it to go within, using the introspective energies to examine their feelings and thoughts and delve deep within their psyche.

While the moon is hidden it's also a powerful time to scry and perform any kind of divination that will uncover your hidden truths, and for getting in touch with your inner wisdom and approaching the Mysteries. This energy helps you explore the darkest recesses of your mind and your heart, and acknowledge your passions, your fears and your anger so you can release them to the approaching light.

This is a time to rest and renew your strength, and also to evaluate your life and your progress. The powerful, deep and transforming energy of the dark moon is an internalised vibration, so be aware of your thoughts, avoiding focusing on negativity or self-loathing in case you manifest the fears you're supposed to banish. The dark moon celebrates the crone, so invoke the energies of Ceridwen, Kali, the Cailleach, Hecate, Baba Yaga or Nephthys to help you descend to your metaphorical underworld and examine the layers of your subconscious.

Eclipses of the Moon and Sun

Lunar and solar eclipses, while fairly rare, also affect the energies of the universe, and our emotions. An eclipse occurs when one celestial body obscures another, either partially or fully. Because of the angle of their orbits, the sun, moon and earth rarely align precisely, which is the condition required for an eclipse. But when the moon is directly between the other two, which can only happen at the dark moon, it blocks the sun's light from reaching the earth, creating a solar eclipse that makes the sun seem either totally or partially invisible. And when the earth is directly between the sun and the moon, which can only happen at the full moon, the earth blocks the sun's light from reaching the moon, producing a lunar eclipse that dims or even totally obscures the moon for a brief time.

Energetically, eclipses create opportunities for change. They can sometimes push you a bit further than you wanted to go, forcing you to move forward and continue along your path. To some they are a wake-up call, nudging you on and making sure you don't lose sight of your dream. A solar eclipse, when the moon blocks the sun, is considered a peak of feminine power, and gets you in touch with your intuition. It is the perfect time to take stock of where you're at and examine your inner self. The energy of a lunar eclipse, when the earth blocks the sun and plunges the moon into darkness, gives you the strength to be honest, to yourself and others, about who you are, and to move forward without fear of judgement.

January

The first month of the Gregorian calender was named in honour of Janus, the Roman god of gates, archways and doors. Janus was the custodian of transitions from old to new, and was depicted with two faces, each looking in different directions, which symbolises the power to reflect on the past year while looking forward to the coming one. The Roman calendar on which ours is based was introduced by Romulus, the first ruler of Rome, around 750BCE. It had 10 months of around 30 days each, followed by a period of winter that had no name. Frustrated by variations in the length of the years, Numa Pompilius, the second Roman king, made revisions around 700BCE. He added the months Februarius and Januarius after December, creating a 12-month calendar. In 46BCE dictator Julius Caesar reformed it further, adding the leap year rule to keep it in line with the seasons, and declaring January the first month. **January's flowers:** Carnations, associated with pure love and remembrance, and snowdrops, a symbol of hope. **Birthstone:** Garnet, which boosts passion, energy and courage, inspires fidelity and constancy and is the stone of commitment.

1st New Year's Day. In the western world this is the first day of a new year, and it's a good time to set goals and make resolutions for the future. It's also **World Peace Day** in the Vatican, Global Family Day, and was the **Feast of Hera**, the Greek goddess of love and marriage.

2nd Inanna's Day. This is celebrated as the birthday of Inanna, the Sumerian goddess of love, fertility and warfare, and queen of heaven. In the Voudon religion it's **Casse Gateau**, Breaking the Cakes, where offerings of food are made to the deities. And in South Africa it's **Kaapse Klopse**, the Cape Minstrel Carnival, which marks the new year.

5th Twelfth Night, or Epiphany Eve, is a night of merrymaking that marks the coming of the Epiphany and the end of the Christmas festivities. The tree comes down, special foods are eaten, and in some countries kids run through the streets to scare away evil spirits.

6th Epiphany. This Christian feast day celebrates the coming of the Magi and the revelation of Jesus as God in human form. In Germany and Italy it's the **Day of Light**, a holy day dedicated to their goddesses.

7th Sekhmet's Day. A time to honour the lion-headed Egyptian sun goddess and patron of healing, strength, war and courage. It's also **Christmas** in the Eastern Orthodox Church, where religious festivals are still determined by the Julian calendar. This is currently 13 days behind the Gregorian, so holy days occur 13 days after the same one in the Western Church. Next century it will grow to a 14-day difference.

8th Midwives Day. In several European countries this is a day when midwives are honoured, men stay at home to do the chores and women relax with friends. The goddess Hecate is worshipped as the Divine Midwife, and it's also sacred to **Justita**, Roman goddess of justice.

9th Feast of the Black Nazarene. A procession with a black Jesus statue takes place in Manila, the Philippines, with pilgrims coming from around the country to touch it. It's also the eve of the **Voodoo Festival** in the West African town of Ouidah, the historic centre of this faith.

13th Vogel Gryff. In Basel, Switzerland, this Harry Potter-sounding festival is held on the 13th, 20th or 27th to chase away winter. Dating back to the 16th century, it involves a procession of a wild man, a lion and a griffin, mythological symbols with great significance in the town. It's also the Hindu bonfire festival of **Lohri**, a solar event dedicated to fire, fertility and winter's end. People petition the gods for abundance with prayers, food and other offerings, and gifts are exchanged.

14th Ganga Sagar Melar. At Sagar Island in India, Hindu pilgrims ritually bathe at the place where the holy Ganges River meets the sea. This is also the day of the Hindu festival of **Makara Sankranthi**, which celebrates the transition of the sun. The goddess of knowledge is honoured, respects are paid to departed ancestors, and beautiful kites are flown to symbolise the act of people reaching towards god.

16th Religious Freedom Day. In the US, this marks the anniversary of the 1786 passing of the Virginia Statute of Religious Freedom, drafted by Thomas Jefferson, which is the framework for the religious freedom clauses in the First Amendment of their constitution.

21st Rowan Month begins. In the ancient Celtic calendar, years were divided into 13 months, which were each associated with a sacred tree. Rowan tree people are passionate, yet they often hide this beneath a cooler facade. They are highly principled, visionary and unique, and prepared to fight for their beliefs. They're pioneering, with a philosophical, keen-minded intellect, and will achieve much. They can be misunderstood though, and need to be clear when communicating. This is also **Saint Agnes's Day**, dedicated to the third century virgin-martyr and patron saint of young girls. On Saint Agnes's Eve, women believed they would dream of their future husband, and often slipped a piece of bridal cake under their pillow to assist their visions.

25th Saint Tatiana's Day. In Russia, this is the feast day of Tatiana, a second century Christian martyr and beloved patroness of students. It's also **Burns Night** in Scotland, a celebration of the life and work of poet and national treasure Robert Burns, born on this day in 1759.

26th Australia Day. The country's national day, it commemorates English settlement in 1788 with fireworks, award presentations, concerts and beer. It's also known as Survival Day for the effect this had on the Aboriginal inhabitants. It is also **Republic Day** in India.

30th Festival of Peace. This was a Roman holy day dedicated to Pax, the goddess of peace, as well as **Feriae Senentiva**, the Feast of Spring.

◊ In Japan, the first three days of January are dedicated to **Hatsumode**, the first shrine or temple visit of the year. Kimonos are worn, offerings are made and prayers are said requesting happiness and prosperity.

◊ On the January full moon the Kelani Procession, **Duruthu Perahera**, is held in Colombo, Sri Lanka, to honour the visit of the Buddha in the fifth century BCE, with displays of ancient traditions and culture.

◊ On the second Monday in January, the Japanese celebrate **Seijinshiki**, Coming of Age Day, for those who will turn 20 that year. It honours the rebirth of the young into responsible adults. And on the second Sunday in January it is **Yamayaki**, a sacred fire festival celebrated in Nara with one of the world's biggest bonfires.

◊ At the end of January the **Kiruna Snow Fest** is held in Kiruna, Sweden. Stargazing, northern lights viewing and snow sculpting takes place.

◊ The last Tuesday marks the **Up-Helly-Aa Festival** in Scotland's Shetland Islands, which celebrates the rebirth of the sun at Yule and spring's return. It's a fire festival, at which a Viking longship is torched and much merrymaking takes place to celebrate their Norse heritage.

◊ **Chinese New Year** is the main holiday of the year for more than one quarter of the world's population, and kicks off a 15-day period of celebrations, festivities, ancient rituals, gift giving, family gatherings, feasts, purification and prayer. New Year's Day falls on the second new moon after the winter solstice, between January 21 and February 21.

◊ On the 23rd day of the 12th lunar month of the Chinese year, just before Chinese New Year, it's the **Day of the Kitchen God**. The deity Zao Jun, who protects each home and the people who live there, makes his report to the gods on the behaviour of the family over the past year.

February

The second month of the year was called Februarius, from the word februare, to purify, as it was the Roman month of purification, sacred to the goddess Juno Februa. It is the only month with 28 days, as opposed to 30 or 31, and is the one that gains an extra day in leap years. This usually occurs every fourth year, except for century years, which only gain a day if divisible by 400 (so 2000 was a leap year, but 1800 and 1900 were not). **February's flowers:** Violets, primroses and irises, all purple blooms that represent purity, devotion and virtue. **Birthstone:** Amethyst, which helps relieve stress and emotional issues, and is used in meditation and to increase psychic abilities.

1st Lughnasadh. Many pagans in the southern hemisphere mark this autumnal harvest festival today, while in the north they celebrate **Imbolc**, the festival of the goddess Bridie and the first day of spring. It's also **Saint Bridget's Day**, the feast day of the Irish saint who was so closely linked to the goddess Bridie that she shares her holy day.

2nd Candlemas. The Christian church transformed the candle festival of Imbolc into Candlemas, which is also marked with candlelit processions. In Ancient Rome it was **Juno Februa Day**, a celebration of the Roman goddess of motherhood and marriage, who was honoured with candles as part of the Lupercalia festival. The Pope changed it into the Purification of the Blessed Virgin, also marked with a candle ceremony, to commemorate the day Mary became "clean" again 40 days after giving birth. In the USA and Canada it's **Groundhog Day**.

3rd Setsubun. In Japan, this Shinto festival is celebrated on the eve of the first day of spring, with special purification rituals performed to cleanse away the negativity of the old year, and bean throwing to drive out evil spirits. Ceremonies are held to ward off evil, with people dressing up to confuse the spirits. Shinto is an ancient nature-based religion where all the deities of heaven and earth are worshipped.

6th Aphrodite's Day. Tributes were made on this day to the Greek goddess of love and beauty, who is still beloved of pagans today. It's also **Waitangi Day** in New Zealand, which commemorates the signing of the Treaty of Waitangi, the country's founding document, in 1840.

9th Apollo's Day. Sacred to Apollo, the Greek god of the sun and patron of light, truth, prophecy, healing and the arts. In Christian times the day was transformed into the Feast Day of Saint Apollonia.

11th Gobnait's Day. This sixth century Irish saint, the patron of bee keepers, is attributed with miracle healings and thwarting an attack by loosing her bees on the enemy. She is believed to be the Christianisation of an earlier fertility goddess symbolised by a bee. It's also the **Feast Day of Our Lady of Lourdes**, after the Virgin Mary allegedly appeared in a vision to a schoolgirl at a grotto in Lourdes, France, on this day in 1858. Millions have made a pilgrimage of healing to the spot, which had been a sacred goddess shrine for centuries.

12th Artemis's Day. A festival dedicated to Artemis, Greek goddess of the hunt, wild animals, wilderness, fertility and healing. She became the goddess of the moon, while her brother Apollo became god of the sun. It's also **Darwin Day**, marking the birthday of naturalist Charles Darwin and his incredible achievements in science and biology.

14th Valentine's Day. The day of love is based on the ancient Roman spring festival, the **Lupercalia**, where rituals were held to purify the city, both physically and energetically, and increase health and fertility. There was also a matchmaking tradition where single women's names were placed in an urn so men could draw one out and pair off with them for a year of trial marriage. This was converted by Christians to Valentine's Day, named for Saint Valentine, with saints names replacing the women's and people encouraged to honour the saint they drew out. It's also sacred to the Norse god **Vali**, the archer.

15th Nirvana Day. Also known as Parinirvana, this is the celebration of the Buddha's death and his attainment of enlightenment – nirvana. Buddhists visit temples, reflect on the Buddha's words and consider their lives and how they can gain the perfect peace of nirvana.

17th Kali's Day. This day is sacred to the Hindu goddess of life and death, who represents destruction as well as positive change, and rules over time and endings. The consort of the god Shiva, she also has a benevolent, maternal aspect. It is also **Random Acts of Kindness Day**, so perform acts of kindness for friends, strangers and yourself.

18th Ash Month begins. Ash tree people are reliable, trustworthy and faithful. They are also vivacious, intelligent and demanding, and don't like to be criticised. They are very grounded but still open to spirituality and destiny, with an intuitive streak and a deep connection to their emotions. They are artistic, inspiring others with the way they see the world, and are ambitious yet humble, a positive combination.

24th Dragobete. This Romanian holiday, known as the day when the birds are betrothed, is similar to Valentine's Day. It's a spring festival, so flowers are picked and ice is melted to make love potions. In Mexico it is **Flag Day**, commemorating the 1821 treaty proclaiming the country's independence, while they celebrate **Dia de la Constitucion**, marking the creation of a constitution, on the first Monday in February.

25th Baika-sai. In Japan, geishas host a tea ceremony beneath the plum blossoms in honour of Sugawara Michizane, a ninth century scholar, poet and politician deified as the god of study after he died.

26th Mut's Day. A festival to honour the Egyptian goddess of protection and spiritual development, known as the divine mother. She was the wife of the creator god Amun and mother of Khonsu, the moon god.

27th Polar Bear Day. A celebration of these majestic creatures, who are native to the North Pole areas and are threatened by pollution, poaching, global warming, industrial accidents and loss of habitat.

29th Leap Day. There is a tradition that women may propose marriage on a leap day – it was even legislated in Scotland in the 13th century. Olympic Games and US presidential elections are held in Leap Years.

◊ In mid-February, the snow festival of **Yuki Matsuri** takes place in Japan, attracting more than two million people a year.

◊ **Ash Wednesday**, the first day of Lent, falls on the seventh Wednesday before Easter, which can be as early as February 4 or as late as March 10. This 40-day Christian festival of purification and denial (Sundays aren't included in the count), is preceded by **Shrove Tuesday**, also known as Pancake Day, Mardi Gras and Carnaval (Latin for farewell to meat), the last fling before Lent begins. On the Saturday before Lent the famous **Brazilian Carnaval**, aka Rio's Mardi Gras, takes place.

◊ The Hindu festival **Vasant Panchami** falls on the first day of spring, usually in February. It honours Saraswati, goddess of learning, music, knowledge and art, and the wife of Brahma. Temples are visited, prayers are recited, spring is welcomed and the god of love is worshipped.

◊ The most important holiday in Tibet is **Losar**, the Tibetan New Year, which falls on the first day of their lunar year, which is the day of the new moon in late January or February. It often, but not always, coincides with Chinese New Year. Rituals of purification and ceremonies to usher in the new year and its new energy take place, people visit their lama, take offerings to the temples and spend time with family. Another festival takes place two weeks later, on the full moon, to end Losar and celebrate the great deeds of the Buddha with blessing lamps.

March

In the Roman calendar, the month of Martius was originally the first month of the year, and its first day fell on the spring equinox, which now falls around the 21st in the Gregorian calendar. It was named for Mars, the powerful god of war, agriculture and the season of spring. According to legend he was also the father of Romulus, the founder of Rome, and thus the protector of the city. Several festivals in honour of this god took place throughout the month. His Greek counterpart was the war god Ares, who gave his name to the first zodiac sign of the year, which began on the first day of Martius. **March's flowers:** Daffodils and jonquils, which represent spring, new beginnings, desire and happiness. **Birthstone:** Aquamarine, known as mermaids treasure, which symbolises courage and serenity, boosts spiritual harmony and balance, improves communication and releases fear. Another gem associated with March is the bloodstone, which imparts courage.

1st Baba Marta. This was an Eastern European celebration of warmer weather and wellbeing. Baba Marta, Grandmother March, is a mythical old woman who brings the end of winter and the start of spring. In Ancient Rome on this day, the **Vestal Virgins** performed a ritual in the Temple of Vesta, rekindling the sacred fire on the first day of their year. It was also **Matronalia**, the festival of the mother goddess Juno, while in Greece they honoured their matriarch Hera, queen of the gods.

2nd Holy Wells Day. A time to honour Ceadda, a Celtic goddess of sacred wells and healing springs. In Scotland it's also known as **Day of Crows**, as the behaviour of these birds is considered prophetic.

3rd Hina Matsuri. In Japan, the Doll Festival is celebrated to wish young girls a successful life and pray for their happiness. Dolls which represent different virtues are displayed and ceremonies performed.

4th Rhiannon's Day. Sacred to the Celtic goddess of inspiration, transformation, wisdom and magic, who has links to the fairies and is deeply connected to nature and animals. Modern pagans invoke this lunar deity for help with manifestation and when in need of a muse.

6th Mars's Day. The festival of Mars, god of war and agriculture and father of the Roman people, when household gods were venerated.

8th International Women's Day. A celebration of the achievements and struggles of women, this has been observed since the early 1900s, and is marked in different ways depending on the country.

13th A day of luck. For magical practitioners, 13 is a sacred number, and when combined with the third month of the year it becomes even more charged with magic and power. If it's a Friday too, all the better.

14th White Day. In Japan, this is a day of love when men give gifts of chocolate or jewellery to the special women in their life. A month earlier, on Valentine's Day, it is the women who buy the presents.

16th Bacchanalia. In Ancient Rome this wild pagan festival was held in honour of Bacchus, the god of wine, fertility and agriculture, at the time of the grape harvest. Today the term bacchanalia refers to drunken revelry, but it was a series of religious rites and Mysteries.

17th Saint Patrick's Day. While this day is celebrated with drinking in the mould of the Bacchanalia, it began as a feast day for the patron saint of Ireland, who converted countless pagans to Christianity.

18th Alder Month begins. Alder tree people are powerful, confident and independent. They're courageous, protective and kind, but can also be impatient, restless and rash. Many of them have great psychic insight, they get on with almost everyone, make great leaders and will passionately follow their own path. The day is also dedicated to **Sheela-na-Gig**, an old pagan fertility goddess whose image was carved into Celtic churches and castles to ward off death and evil spirits.

19th Athena's Day. Celebrated as the birthday of the Greek goddess of wisdom, war, healing and art, and her Roman counterpart **Minerva**. It's also **Saint Joseph's Day**, in honour of the Virgin Mary's husband.

20th Mabon. Around this day in the southern hemisphere is the autumn equinox, when light and dark is equal, while in the north it is the spring equinox, celebrated by pagans as Ostara. It is also the feast day of the Voudon deity **Papa Legba**, who rules healing, protection, spirit work, fate, crossroads and the sun, and **World Storytelling Day**, highlighting the significance of oral storytelling as an art form.

21st Day for the Elimination of Racial Discrimination. This global event marks the anniversary of the day in 1960 that police in South Africa opened fire at a peaceful demonstration against apartheid, killing 69. It raises awareness of the effect of racism in all communities.

25th Lady Day. The Feast of the Annunciation of the Virgin, this was originally set on the spring equinox, and is a Christian quarter day. It celebrates the revelation to Mary that she would conceive the son of God. Until 1752 it was the beginning of the legal year in England.

28th Quan Yin's Day. Birthday of the Buddhist goddess of compassion and love, who protects women and children and awakens our abilities.

◊ The Hindu spring festival of **Holi**, also called the Festival of Colours, falls on the 15th day of the month of Phalgun each year, a full moon, although the date shifts from late February to March on the western calendar. Bonfires are lit to purify the land and drive out demons, and people throw coloured powders of ayurvedic medicines at each other to boost health, make life more colourful and ward off sorrow.

◊ **Maha Shivratri**, Great Night of Shiva, is a Hindu dark moon festival that falls in February or March, symbolising the wedding of Lord Shiva and the goddess Parvati. Devotees fast, make offerings, do penance for their sins and light sacred fires that they watch all night.

◊ In mid March in Kyoto, Japan, **Higashiyama Hanatoro**, Romantic Flower Lantern Lane Festival, takes place, with lanterns lining the streets and forests, temples lit up, and geishas dancing and singing.

◊ In Japan, Vernal Equinox Day, known as **Shunbun no Hi**, falls around March 20. This Shinto festival, a national holiday, is the middle day of a seven-day period known as Higan, which means the other side of the river of death, and the ancestors are worshipped and tombs visited. It also refers to enlightenment, and is a day of contemplation.

◊ **New Year celebrations** in Persian countries like Iran and Afghanistan are held on the spring equinox, the first day of their month of Farvardin. Called **Norouz**, it begins at the moment of equinox, and acknowledges the new year as well as spring and the awakening of life after the barrenness of winter. It is marked by house cleaning and purification rituals, seed sprouting, new clothes, fire festivals and family picnics.

◊ In Japan, the **Cherry Blossom Festival** of Hanami also takes place around this time, with cherry blossom viewing parties, ancient tea ceremonies, traditional folk music and dance performances as well as food, games, rides, parades, kimono shows and religious ceremonies.

◊ The Jewish festival of Pesach, also called **Passover**, begins on the 15th of their month of Nissan, which falls in late March or early April. It commemorates the exodus from Egypt with rituals and ceremony.

◊ **Earth Hour** falls on the last Saturday in March. It began in Sydney, Australia, in 2007, and has become a global event. For one hour, from 8.30pm, people and corporations turn off the power to save an immense amount of electricity and raise awareness about climate change.

April

In the Roman calendar, the month of Aprilis, originally the second of the year, honoured Venus, the goddess of love, passion, beauty and nature and the partner of the god Mars. The name is believed to come from her Greek counterpart Aphrodite, whose month was called Aphrilis, or from the Latin word aperire, which means to open, referring to the opening up of nature in springtime. **April's flowers:** Daisies, which represent innocence, sentiment and lasting love, and sweetpeas, which signify tender memories and curiosity. **Birthstone:** Diamond, symbolising purity and strength. The fire inside is believed to reflect the flame of love, thus they are still used in engagement rings.

1st April Fool's Day. A day for practical jokes and good humour. The Iranian version, **Sizdah Bedar**, falls on April 1st or 2nd, 12 days after their new year, and marks the end of Norouz. It also involves pranks, as well as picnics and prayers for rain to cleanse people of bad fortune. This day was also sacred to the goddesses **Venus** and **Aphrodite**.

2nd International Children's Book Day. This day was proclaimed to inspire a love of reading in young people, gain attention for kids books and support different children's charities. It is held on the anniversary of beloved Danish storyteller **Hans Christian Andersen**'s birthday.

5th Qingming Festival. This Chinese festival, known as Tomb Sweeping Day or Clear and Bright Festival, is celebrated on the 15th day after the spring equinox. It is a celebration of the rebirth of nature and a time to honour the ancestors. People tend to the graves of departed loved ones and carry willow branches to ward off evil spirits. It's also **Lady Luck Day**, a festival in honour of Fortuna, the old Roman fertility goddess who oversaw good fortune, abundance and prosperity.

7th World Health Day. The UN's World Health Organization created this day to raise awareness of global health issues. In Romania, it's **Blajini**, the day when their blajinies – gentle, kind-hearted ones, like fairies – are honoured with offerings at wells, springs and rivers.

8th Buddha's Birthday. In Japan, a flower festival, Hana Matsuri, marks the birthday of the Buddha on this day, although in other Asian countries it is celebrated on the eighth day of the fourth month of the Chinese lunar calendar. Flowers and offerings are left at temples, free meals are given to the poor, and religious services are performed. It is also **International Day of the Roma**, a celebration of gypsy culture.

13th Songkran. In Thailand, Cambodia and Laos, New Year's Day is called Songkran, and is celebrated from April 13 to April 15. It's a national holiday on which people throw water, exchange gifts, visit their families and do community service at the temple. The Punjabi new year, **Vaisakhi**, is also celebrated on this day, marking the start of spring and the end of the harvest in India. So too is the Burmese New Year Water Festival, **Thingyan**, the country's most important holiday. It runs over three days, and involves temple visits, offerings, flowers, ritual cleansing ceremonies and hair washing. The mythical figure of Thagya Min is said to descend from his celestial abode to record saints and sinners in his book, prophecies are made and people splash water at one another to wash away their sins. This day was also sacred to **Libertas**, the Roman goddess of liberty and freedom.

15th Willow Month begins. Willow tree people are intuitive, empathic and a little mysterious, as they are influenced by the moon. They are tenacious, resourceful and honest, and love to travel and dream. They can be moody and restless, but are very loving and appreciate beauty around them. They are patient, which sometimes leads to hesitation, intelligent and creative, and blossom when they trust their intuition.

16th Saint Bernadette's Day. Marie-Bernarde Soubirous, the girl who saw the visions of a "lady" at Lourdes in France – which the Catholic Church confirmed was the Virgin Mary – died on this day in 1879, and was canonised a decade later. It's now her feast day.

21st Kartini Day. In Indonesia, the birthday of 19th century women's rights heroine Raden Ajeng Kartini is a national holiday. Denied schooling once she turned 12, she started a school for girls and lobbied for educational rights and equality for women. The day is marked with celebrations, exhibitions and cultural performances.

22nd Earth Day. Horrified by the Santa Barbara oil spill in 1969 and the degradation of nature, a US senator called for an international day to inspire awareness of and appreciation for the earth. The next year Earth Day was launched, marking the beginning of the environmental movement. In magical traditions it's **Earth Spirit Day**, when pagans perform earth healing rituals and work with the elementals of the land.

23rd Saint George's Day. Famous for a legend that he slayed a dragon – the dragon symbolising a pagan cult he converted – this Roman soldier was venerated as a Christian martyr when he died in 303, and became the patron saint of England and many other countries. It's also **World Book Day**, a UNESCO-created event that honours books and reading, particularly in developing nations where literacy is low.

25th Anzac Day. A public holiday in Australia and New Zealand, this honours members of the army who fought at Gallipoli in Turkey during World War I. The Anzac legend is now part of the national identity. It's also **World Penguin Day**, as these creatures native to the southern hemisphere – they're found in Antarctica, South Africa, Australia and New Zealand – begin their annual migration. And in Portugal it's **Freedom Day**, the anniversary of their Carnation Revolution.

27th Freedom Day. In South Africa, this is a public holiday celebrating freedom and commemorating the first post-apartheid elections, held on this day in 1994, the first time all people of voting age were allowed to vote. **UnFreedom Day** is also marked by some, in protest for those, particularly the poor, who still have few rights.

28th Festival of Flowers. In Ancient Rome the Floralia began at this time, a festival in honour of Flora, the goddess of fertility and flowers – hence the name flora for plants (and for a fairy in *Sleeping Beauty*). The Floralia was celebrated with dancing, drinking, drama and flowers, and offerings of milk and honey were made in the temples.

30th Walpurgis Night. In many parts of Europe, Walpurgisnacht (Witches Night) was a Norse festival to farewell the long Scandinavian winter. Bonfires were lit to ward off dark spirits and welcome the return of the sun, and sacred fires and merrymaking continue to this day. Christians transformed it to Walpurga Night in honour of Saint Walpurga, an eighth century Saxon princess who became a nun, and whose birthday was on this day. It is also **Mange les Morts**, in the Voudon tradition, a day for feeding the spirits of the family ancestors.

◊ In Switzerland, **Sechselauten**, the Six Ringing Festival, falls in early April. Pageants, processions, bonfires and bells signify winter is over.

◊ The Christian festival of **Easter** marks the death and resurrection of Jesus, and is an important event on the religious calender. Easter Sunday falls on the first Sunday after the full moon on or after the vernal equinox, which means it can fall as early as March 22 and as late as April 25. **Orthodox Easter** sometimes coincides with western Easter (in 2010, 2011 and 2014), but not always. Easter Sunday in the Orthodox Church can fall as early as April 4 and as late as May 8.

◊ Across Asia, **Hanuman Jayanti**, the birthday of the Hindu monkey god Hanuman Ji, is celebrated on the 15th day of the month of Chaitra, a full moon, which often falls in April. This god represents strength and energy. Prayers are recited to him, sacred texts are read, and there's a period of fasting that ends with a huge vegetarian feast.

May

The Roman month of Maius was named for Maia, an earth goddess who symbolised life, love, rebirth, fertility and warmth. She was also known as Maia Maiestas, Maia the Majestic, to indicate how powerful she was. She was married to the fire god Vulcan, and later linked to the Greek goddess of the same name, one of the seven sisters who formed the constellation of the Pleiades. **May's flowers:** Lilies of the valley, which represent happiness, humility and completion, and sunflowers, symbolising joy and sunshine. **Birthstone:** Emerald, which imparts wisdom, patience, love and fidelity to those who wear it.

1st Samhain. Today in the southern hemisphere many pagans celebrate this festival, and the first day of winter, while in the north it is the fertility festival of **Beltane** and the start of summer. The Irish goddess **Lasair**, which translates as flame, was also celebrated on this day. She was the oldest of three sisters representing the harvest cycle, and oversaw the growing, ripening and harvesting of crops. When Ireland became Christianised she was transformed into a saint. It's also **May Day** and **Labour Day**, an international day of solidarity among workers, and a festival dedicated to the Ancient Roman fertility goddess **Maia**.

2nd Yashodhara's Day. In India, the Buddha's wife is honoured on this day. When her husband left her on the day their child was born to seek nirvana, she echoed his spiritual search with an austere life, and became a Buddhist nun on the day he attained enlightenment.

4th Fairy Day. Fairies and their bright, sometimes mischievous magic are synonymous with Beltane, and they've long been honoured on this day, with offerings left out so they won't do any harm. In modern times the World Fairy Festival runs on the Saturday closest to this day.

6th Inghean Bhuidhe's Day. The Irish goddess Inghean Bhuidhe, which translates as bloom of youth, was the middle of three sisters representing the harvest cycle. She had a nurturing mother goddess energy, and symbolised the ripening of the crops, fertility and the start of summer. She was later turned into a Christian saint, and had her feast day today, the first day of summer in the northern hemisphere.

8th Flora's Dance. In Cornwall, England, this is Furry Dance Day, where villagers dance in honour of the Horned God. It is one of the oldest British customs still alive today, and celebrates the end of winter and the virility of the pagan lord of nature and the wild.

10th Mother's Day. In Mexico, this celebration of motherhood is set on this day each year, but in many countries, including Australia, the US and South America, it falls on the second Sunday of the month.

13th Hawthorn Month begins. Hawthorn tree people are innovative, full of ideas and can adapt easily to change. They don't always show their inner self, and often burn with passion under a cool exterior. They can be very serious in business, and are dependable, tough and clever, and protective of family and friends. They're born performers, talented and expressive, with a gift of the gab and good listening skills.

15th Aoi Matsuri. The Hollyhock Leaf Crest Festival is one of Japan's most important, dating from the sixth century, when the emperor made offerings to gain the favour of the harvest deities. Aoi (hollyhock) leaves were believed to protect against natural disasters. In Ancient Rome, **Mercury**, the messenger of the gods and patron of communication, wisdom and travel, was also honoured on this day with a festival, the Mercuralia, as was his Greek counterpart **Hermes** and the Roman goddess **Maia**, who became identified as Mercury's mother.

16th Saint Brendan's Day. It's the feast day of the sixth century Irish monk who, according to legend, navigated his way from the west coast of Ireland to the Americas, centuries before Columbus and in a tiny craft like a canoe, seeking paradise. He also founded a monastery.

20th Plynteria. A festival in honour of Athena, the Greek goddess of wisdom, battle and heroic endeavour. She was strong, fair and merciful, the wise patron of Athens, whose people built the Parthenon in the fifth century BCE as a temple to worship her. She was a "virgin" goddess – an independent, self-contained, sexually free woman.

21st Maeve's Day. This Celtic deity, reimagined as Mab, queen of the fairies, in modern retellings, was goddess of Ireland's sovereignty and its mystic heart. She helps people recognise their own inner queen.

23rd Declaration of the Bab. This is the anniversary of the founding of the Bahai faith in 1844, when Siyyid Ali Muhammad was revealed as the Bab, leader of this new Persian faith. His mission was to prepare the world for the coming of Bahaullah, the manifestation of God.

26th Sorry Day. In Australia in 1998, a national day of apology was instituted to acknowledge the harm done by the forced removal of Aboriginal children from their families in the early 1900s to 1970. The government finally apologised for its treatment of Aboriginal people and their dispossession from their land on February 13, 2008.

29th Oak Apple Day. Commemorating the restoration of the English monarchy in 1660, this was a day of thanksgiving, and later transformed into Arbour Day, when trees are planted. It had its roots in paganism though – a Garland King would ride through the streets completely disguised in greenery, and oak sprigs were worn and displayed.

30th Joan of Arc Day. Commemoration of a French heroine and military leader who was burnt at the stake on this day in 1431 as a witch and heretic. Twenty-five years later her case was reviewed and she was found innocent and declared a martyr, later being canonised as a saint. It's also a day of remembrance for the Burning Times, and all wise women and healers who were executed for their knowledge.

◊ In the Philippines, the **Flores de Mayo**, Flowers of May, is a month-long celebration held this month in honour of the Virgin Mary. There are religious processions, flower offerings, prayers, beauty pageants, music, dancing and entertainment. A highlight is the **Santa Cruzan**, the Queen of Filipino Festival, in honour of Saint Helen.

◊ The most important Buddhist celebration of the year is **Vesak**, the commemoration of the Buddha's birth, death and enlightenment – although his birthday is honoured earlier in the year. On this day prayers are recited in the temples from early morning, offerings of flowers, candles and incense are made in petition for his love and guidance, and followers reaffirm their faith. They perform charitable deeds and help those less fortunate, and try to joyfully embody their faith as an example to others. Vesak usually takes place in May in the Gregorian calendar, although the date varies – for Theravada Buddhists in countries such as Thailand, Cambodia and Burma, Vesak falls on the full moon of their fifth or sixth month, while for Mahayana Buddhists in countries such as China, Tibet, Japan and Indonesia it's on the full moon of the fourth month of the Chinese calendar.

◊ The **Buddhist Ploughing Festival**, called Raek Na in Thailand, is a celebration commemorating the Buddha's first glimpse of enlightenment as a child. It takes place when the May moon is half full, and involves rituals and offerings, as well as a procession of two white ox pulling a golden plough while young girls scatter seeds, watched over by Buddhist monks sitting beside a towering statue of Lord Buddha.

◊ In the last weekend in May, the **Aalborg Carnival** takes place in Denmark. It's Europe's largest, with up to 25,000 carnivalists in the Grand Parade. It celebrates fantasy and the coming of spring, and transforms the city into a gigantic theatre with the citizens as actors, the street as the stage and the body as a dancing sculpture.

June

The Roman month of Junius, meaning sacred to Juno, was dedicated to the goddess of women, childbirth and protection. She was the wife of Jupiter, king of the gods, so she ruled the other goddesses, and the deity of marriage, which made her month a fortuitous time to wed. **June's flowers:** Honeysuckles, which embody sweetness and love, and roses, which signify purity and love. June is National Rose Month in the US. **Birthstones:** Moonstone, a milky white crystal that holds the energy of the moon and increases psychic visions, enhances intuition and sensitivity and boosts dream awareness and spiritual awakening, as well as the pearl, which represents love and purity.

2nd Ishtar's Day. This was sacred to the Babylonian goddess of love, fertility and rebirth through battle, who was queen of the heavens, a role Isis fulfilled in Egypt. Ishtar was associated with the planet Venus, the morning star, and was the deity of love and war through the ages.

5th World Environment Day. A UN-declared holiday, this aims to improve the state of the environment around the world, stimulate worldwide awareness of the issues and encourage political action.

7th Vestalia. The Ancient Roman festival dedicated to Vesta, the nurturing fire goddess of the home, hearth and purity, began on this day. The temples were ritually purified, and all women could enter the shrine of Vesta, which was usually restricted to the Vestal Virgins.

9th Saint Columba's Day. This sixth century rebel Irish priest warred with a fellow man of the cloth, which led to many deaths, and was exiled from his home shores as punishment. He sailed to the Scottish Isle of Iona, where he founded a monastery and converted many pagans.

10th Oak Month begins. Oak tree people are optimistic, honest and courageous. They don't like change, yet cope well with difficulties by adapting and growing stronger. They have an inner strength and generosity of spirit, and while they sometimes commit too quickly, their unrelenting nature means they will follow through. Like the oak tree they are protective, and speak up for those without a voice.

11th Kamehameha Day. The national day of Hawaii, it commemorates the great warrior, known as Napoleon of the Pacific for his achievements in warfare and diplomacy, who united the islands into a single kingdom and defended indigenous culture against invaders. Floral parades, hula contests, traditional music and festivals take place on this day.

12th Dia dos Namorados. In Brazil they celebrate the Day of the Enamoured, their version of Valentine's Day, on this date, which is the eve of the feast of Saint Anthony, the patron of marriage. Single women perform rituals, called simpatias, in the hope of drawing love to them. It was also the day sacred to **Zeus**, the Greek king of the gods.

15th Saint Vitus's Day. Vitus was a Christian preacher from Sicily, martyred in 303. He allegedly affected many cures, especially in epileptic conditions, and today one involuntary movement disorder has been named Saint Vitus's dance (in Latin, chorea sancti viti) after him. He is the patron saint of young people, actors, comedians, epileptics and dancers, and traditionally it was believed that dancing around his statue on this day would impart a year of good health.

16th Youth Day. In South Africa, this day commemorates the gunning down of black students during the Soweto Uprising of 1976, and the long struggle for equality in education and life under the shadow of apartheid, with a focus on hope and change for the future.

19th Hera's Day. A celebration of the Greek goddess of women and marriage. She was the wife and sister of Zeus, and considered queen of the heavens. Her Roman counterpart was the mother goddess Juno. It is also Burmese freedom activist **Aung San Suu Kyi**'s birthday.

21st Solstice. Around this day in the southern hemisphere it is the winter solstice, the shortest day and the longest night of the year, and the pagan celebration of **Yule**, while in the north it is the summer solstice, the longest day of the year, which is honoured as **Litha.**

22nd Religion vs Science. On this day in 1633, the Holy Office in Rome forced the Italian physicist, mathematician and astronomer Galileo Galilei, now known as the Father of Science, to recant his view that the earth rotates around the sun, rather than vice versa, on pain of torture. Despite being correct, he spent the last years of his life under house arrest on the orders of the Roman Inquisition, accused of heresy, banned from teaching and forbidden to publish his works.

24th Solstice celebrations. In some European countries, this day was chosen to celebrate the summer solstice, despite it falling a few days earlier, and it was marked with revelry and all night partying. The Church declared it **Saint John's Day**, in honour of Saint John the Baptist, in an attempt to outlaw solstice rites, but they weren't entirely successful, as people just started lighting Saint John fires instead. This feast day was unusual as it was on his birthday rather than the date of his death – the latter is acknowledged on August 29.

29th Saint Peter and Saint Paul's Day. The patron saints of Rome, two influential members of the early church, are celebrated together on this day. Peter was a leader of the early Christian church, one of the Twelve Apostles and the first Bishop of Rome, making the Pope his successor. He was martyred around 64CE. Paul was an early Christian missionary and apostle, and is the most influential of the New Testament authors. Both have several holy days attributed to them, but this is a solemnity, the highest degree for a liturgical feast. Traditionally, girls who wanted to dream of their future husband would tie nine keys – symbols of Saint Peter, the gatekeeper of heaven – in their hair on this night and petition the saint to reveal a face. It's also a day sacred to **Papa Legba**, Voudon deity of the crossroads.

30th Blodeuwedd's Day. The Celtic Lady of Flowers and goddess of emergence and inner truths, she assists with clarity and wisdom, and is honoured on her special day with flowers and the use of essences.

◊ In China, summer is considered the most yang season – hot, masculine, powerful – and the **summer solstice** is the peak of its strength. But from this day forward its power begins to wane, marking the movement of the planet into the yin part of the year, which celebrates women, nature and the power of the earth's life force. Traditional customs are observed, with special foods, and a popular saying states: "After eating noodles on the summer solstice day, daylight gets shorter day by day." Many cities have begun turning their lights off on the night of the summer solstice to conserve power.

◊ The ancient Japanese **Rice Transplanting Ceremony**, Mitaue, is held in June. A procession of people in traditional costumes, carrying banners, makes its way to the rice fields, where prayers are offered to the rice god Sanbai-sama. A ceremonial fire is lit, rice seedlings are planted and music and dancing commences. Rice has long been revered across Asia, where the tradition of showering newlyweds with uncooked rice to wish them love and prosperity began.

◊ The two-day Jewish harvest festival of Shavu'ot, also known as the **Festival of Weeks**, marks the giving of the Torah at Mount Sinai, an important historical event. It occurs on the sixth day of the month of Sivan, 49 days after Passover, so it usually falls in late May or June.

◊ In a similar vein, **Pentecost**, which marks the coming of the holy spirit, is celebrated 50 days after Easter, so it falls in May or June. In Britain it was known as Whit Sunday, and churches were dressed with green wreaths and boughs to celebrate nature. Matchmaking was popular at this time, which was considered a good month for weddings.

July

July is the seventh month of the Gregorian calendar, and is based on the Roman month Julius, named in honour of emperor Julius Caesar, who reformed the calendar in 46BCE, creating the Julian calendar which forms the basis of our modern time keeping. Until then the month had been called Quintilis, which means fifth, because it was originally the fifth month of the Roman year. **July's flowers:** Water lilies, which open the heart and bring good fortune, and buttercups, bright and cheerful bursts of sunshine. **Birthstone:** Ruby, a blood red precious stone that represents passion, love, loyalty and a strong heart, physically and emotionally, which stimulates the heart chakra.

1st Tirgan. In Iran, the Rain Festival is celebrated with dancing, singing and poetry recitals, and the tying of rainbow-coloured bands around wrists, which are worn for 10 days then thrown into a stream. Children splash water and jump into streams as a purification ritual. Tirgan is also observed around the world to honour Persian culture.

3rd Ceridwen's Day. A festival to honour the crone goddess, keeper of the cauldron of knowledge, transformation and rebirth, was held on this day. A Celtic deity, Ceridwen symbolises wisdom and crone energy.

4th Independence Day. A celebration of the birth of the United States, when thanks is given to Lady Liberty and patriotism rules. In Rome, feasting marked the **Day of Pax**, in honour of the goddess of peace.

5th Ma'at's Day. In honour of Ma'at, the Egyptian goddess of wisdom and justice. The personification of law and morality, she kept chaos at bay, regulated the cycles of time and balanced the scales of the dead.

7th Tanabata. Also known as the Star Festival, this Japanese holiday sees people writing a wish on a piece of paper and tying it to a bamboo tree, alongside pretty paper decorations in the shape of flowers, animals and stars. In Pamplona, Spain, the most famous **Running of the Bulls** event begins on this day, the feast day of Saint Fermin.

8th Holly Month begins. Holly tree people are affectionate, down to earth and trustworthy, and operate with honesty and integrity. They are supportive, sympathetic, loyal and devoted. They're hardworking, tolerant and logical, and enjoy positions of leadership and power. They are sensitive to criticism – and also to the Otherworld. They can be misconstrued as arrogant, but are simply confident of their abilities.

9th Martyrdom of the Bab. This Bahai holy day commemorates the death by firing squad of the messenger of their faith in 1850, which has been compared by followers to the crucifixion of Christ.

10th Hel's Day. This day is sacred to the Norse goddess of death and the underworld, who was associated with the elder tree and honoured with prayers, roses and black candles. It's also when followers of Indian spiritual guru Meher Baba observe a **Day of Silence**, to mark the day in 1925 that he made a permanent vow of silence.

11th Naadam. In Mongolia, nomadic tribespeople meet in the capital to compete in games – wrestling, horse racing and archery – and drink, feast and dance during this traditional three-day festival. In Ancient Greece the day was sacred to **Khronos**, the god who personified time.

14th Gion Matsuri Festival. This month-long festival commemorates the end of a devastating plague in Kyoto, Japan, in 869CE. The highlights begin on the 14th, with a parade of floats, demonstrations of traditional Shinto performing arts and stalls of sweets. It's also **Bastille Day**, which marks the storming of this Parisian prison in 1789 that started the French Revolution and led to the republic. Parades, fireworks, dancing and parties are all part of the celebrations.

15th Bon Festival. The Buddhist Feast of Lanterns has been celebrated in Japan for centuries. People make offerings at family graves, bonfires burn to welcome the ancestors, and lanterns are sent down the river to guide the spirits of recently departed loved ones. **Rosalia**, the Roman festival of roses, which was sacred to Venus, goddess of love, also took place at this time, as did Rosa Mundi, the **Festival of the Rose of the World**, in honour of the mother goddess. Roses were placed on shrines and in front of statues, with appeals for healing, love and forgiveness.

17th Procession for Amaterasu. In Japan, the Shinto sun goddess is celebrated with street processions. All light is thought to emanate from her, and she is renowned for her warmth and compassion.

19th Azarni, Martyrs' Day. In Burma, this day marks the assassination of the country's founding father, General Aung San, and six of his cabinet members, in 1947. His daughter Aung San Suu Kyi continues his fight for equality – she was elected prime minister, but has been under house arrest more than 13 years, so never served. She's won many awards for her non-violent struggle under a military dictatorship.

20th Friendship Day. In South America this is a day to celebrate friendship and give thanks for all the wonderful people in your life.

22nd Saint Mary Magdalene's Day. A celebration of the life of the other Mary, known as a devoted disciple of Jesus. Although she was maligned as a sinner, she transformed into a penitent and then a saint.

23rd Saint Brigit's Day. The patron saint of Sweden, not to be confused with the Irish Saint Bridget, she founded the order of Brigittine nuns in the 14th century. It was also the time of the **Neptunalia**, a festival in honour of Neptune, Roman god of the sea and of water.

25th Latiaran's Day. The Irish goddess Latiaran was the youngest of three sisters who represented the harvest cycle – she was the crone who oversaw the death of the growing season, but was later Christianised as a saint. The Egyptian queen **Hatshepsut**, who lived in the 15th century BCE and was the first female pharaoh, was honoured on this day, as was **Saint James**, one of the Twelve Apostles and patron of the Camino pilgrimage across Spain, and **Saint Christopher**, patron of travellers.

27th Osiris's Day. This Egyptian god ruled the earth with his beloved wife Isis and taught the people agriculture, then later became god of the underworld, overseeing the phases of life, death and rebirth.

28th Horus's Day. The only child of Isis and Osiris, this Egyptian god represented divine kingship and was protector of the pharaohs. He symbolised new beginnings, the rising of the sun and responsibility.

29th Set's Day. The Egyptian god of chaos and disorder became the principle of evil, but was also seen as a balancing force against good.

30th Isis's Day. The Egyptian queen of the heavens and great mother of all creation, she's associated with healing, divination and magic. Parallels have been drawn between her and the Virgin Mary.

31st Nephthys's Day. An Egyptian deity of the dead who comforted those in mourning, she was considered the mother of Anubis, god of the dead. She and Isis were beloved sisters who possessed great magic.

◊ Hindus celebrate **Guru Purnima** on the full moon of their month of Ashad, which falls in July or August. It's sacred to the memory of the sage Vyasa, and a vital day for farmers, heralding the life-giving rains.

◊ The Jewish period of mourning known as **The Three Weeks** takes place between the 17th of Tammus and the 9th of Av on the Hebrew calendar, which usually falls in July and August. No weddings or other celebrations take place, to mark the destruction of the holy temple and the physical exile and spiritual displacement believers endured.

August

The eighth month of the year was originally named Sextilis, Latin for six, because it was the sixth month of the old Roman calendar. In 8BCE it was renamed in honour of emperor Augustus Caesar, and an extra day was taken from February and added to it so it had the same importance as Julius Caesar's month. **August's flowers:** Poppies, which represent remembrance, strength of character and grace, and gladioli, which symbolise sincerity and generosity. **Birthstone:** Peridot, a green crystal known to the Romans as evening emerald, which is a powerful cleanser and purifier, both physically and emotionally, and helps to release guilt, resentment and negativity and bring peace.

1st Imbolc. In the southern hemisphere pagans celebrate the first day of spring around this time, while in the north it's the harvest festival of **Lughnasadh** and the first day of autumn.

5th Hazel Month begins. Hazel tree people are clever and organised, with an urge to learn. The hazel represents wisdom, poetic knowledge and intuition, and those born under this sign have intellect, logic, strong recall and efficiency. They have a creative energy that fires up their work or favourite projects, but must learn patience and how to let go of their need for control in order to achieve all they're capable of.

6th Hiroshima Day. A day of peace marches and vigils held to commemorate the dropping of the first atomic bomb, which landed on the Japanese city of Hiroshima on this day in 1945. It helped end World War II, but killed 70,000 people instantly, and that many again through exposure to the deadly radiation. Known as Hiroshima Peace Ceremony Day in the Shinto religion, and Atomic Bomb Day in the US. It was also the **Festival of Thoth**, honouring the Egyptian god of wisdom and truth, who's credited with inventing language, writing, magic and religion. He was a moon god, and the masculine counterpart of Ma'at.

8th Blessed Mary MacKillop's Day. A feast day for Australia's first would-be saint, who founded the Sisters of Saint Joseph of the Sacred Heart, dedicated to educating the poor. It's also sacred to **Venus**, the goddess of love and beauty, and **Saint Dominic**, patron of astronomers.

9th Day of the World's Indigenous People. A day that honours the achievements of indigenous peoples, and aims to find solutions to some of the problems faced by them in areas such as culture, education, health, human rights, the environment and economic development.

10th Merlin's Day. The ultimate druid, the magician Merlin represents the wise old sage archetype. He's a psychic visionary and favourite of Celtic legends, and can be invoked by people who want to increase their psychic skills and connection to the ancient power of the land.

12th Youth Day. An international celebration of young people, this day was initiated to promote intergenerational understanding and encourage people under 24 to start acting to change the world.

13th Hecate's Day. A day to honour the Ancient Greek goddess of the crossroads, witchcraft, illumination and the moon. Offerings of honeycakes and mushrooms are still left out for her in Greece, and modern witches revere her as a triple goddess of wisdom and change. It's also **Left Handers Day**, to promote understanding of the challenges lefties face among a right-handed majority. Prominent lefties include Barack Obama, Angelina Jolie, Joan of Arc and tennis star Rafael Nadal, who writes with his right hand but plays tennis with his left.

15th Vesta's Day. A time sacred to the Roman goddess of hearth and home, guardian of the sacred flame, and today a deity invoked for protection and harmony around the home. It's also the **Assumption of Mary**, a holy day marking when Mary was taken into heaven.

16th Gozan no Okuribi. This traditional bonfire event is part of the Festival of the Ancestors. A huge bonfire is lit on each of the five mountains surrounding the city of Kyoto in Japan, three in the shape of kanji, one in the shape of a boat and one as a Shinto shrine gate. The fires guide souls and protect against evil, and drinking water that reflects the light of the flames is believed to prevent paralysis.

17th Diana's Day. A day sacred to the Roman goddess Diana, moon maiden and huntress, who was associated with wild animals, woodland and oak groves. She was also considered a divine midwife who oversaw healthy pregnancies and painless childbirth. Today many pagans still revere her, and there is a branch, Dianic Witchcraft, named for her, characterised by an exclusive focus on the divine as feminine.

19th Vinalia. A festival in honour of Athena, Greek goddess of wisdom, war, healing and art, and her Roman counterpart **Minerva**, in their aspect as protectors of gardens and vineyards and bestowers of plenty.

24th Exu's Day. Those who follow the Brazilian religion of Candomble honour Exu at this time. He is the messenger who takes people's prayers to the heavens and the warrior god of mischief and judgement, who is honoured with rum, sweets, toys, dancing and rituals.

26th Fujiyoshida Fire Festival. In Japan, people create a shrine to the goddess Konohansakuyahime and carry it through the streets, which are illuminated with lanterns and sacred fires, in the hope that the goddess will stop Mount Fuji from erupting. It marks the end of summer and the climbing season, and is a time of thanksgiving.

30th Day of the Disappeared. A day that commemorates political prisoners who've been taken into custody by governments but had their whereabouts denied, which aims to raise awareness of their plight.

31st Hathor's Day. The birthday of the Egyptian protector goddess and mother of the pharaohs, who ruled love, joy and music. She was associated with the Nile and thus fertility, and had a mother aspect.

◊ The full moon in August is the date of the **Hungry Ghost Festival**, Chung Yuan, in China. People leave food and other offerings out for the souls of their departed loved ones, who they believe are let out of purgatory on this day to receive sustenance in the land of the living.

◊ Many countries mark the Buddhist **Festival of Bon** in August, which takes place in Japan a month earlier. Kyu Bon, Old Bon, is celebrated by more traditional communities on the 15th day of the seventh month of the old lunar calendar, which often falls in August. It is similar to the Mexican observance of **el Dia de los Muertos**, with people visiting family burial sites, honouring the ancestors with offerings and holding reunions. Small bonfires called mukae-bi, or welcoming flame, are lit to guide the spirits home for the day, as well as hundreds of lanterns.

◊ On the full moon that falls during the Hindu month of Shraavana, which usually occurs in August, is the **Raksha Bandhan** festival, which means bond of protection in Hindi. It celebrates the relationship between brothers and sisters with gifts, feasts and ancient rituals. On this day women tie a Rakhi, a sacred thread, on the wrists of their brother or a male friend, expressing their love, which is returned with a promise of responsibility for her protection. In India, this thread is considered stronger than iron chains to bind people together.

◊ Several festivals take place in Nepal in August. They honour Lord Krishna's birthday at **Krishnastami**, a day of prayers and worship in the temples which begins with a vigil through the night. They perform autumn rituals to invoke protection for their farms and their animals, warding off evil spirits and requesting prosperity and abundance. They also celebrate the festival of **Gai Jatra**, the procession of cows, where people tell jokes, dress as cows and try to lighten the grief of loss. At night they dress up with masks and sing and perform mock theatre.

September

The Ancient Romans named this month Septem, their word for seven, because it was originally the seventh month of their year. It's one of only four months with 30 days, and September 1st always falls on the same day of the week as December 1st. It is the month of the second equinox, so it's a time of balance and harmony. **September's flower:** Asters, daisy-like blooms linked to the goddess Venus, which symbolise love, patience and elegance. **Birthstone:** Sapphire, known as the wisdom stone, which represents truth, calmness and repentance, and strengthens intuition and deep thought while repelling negativity.

2nd Vine Month begins. Vine people are open, forgiving, emotional and sensual, with a great enthusiasm for life and love. They can be changeable and unpredictable, but they see the good in people and inspire harmony and stability between others. People often underestimate their skills, but they are charming and confident, and have the Midas touch in transforming a situation to better suit them.

4th Rhiannon's Day. An autumnal feast day for the Celtic goddess of inspiration, transformation and the moon. Her name means Great Queen, and she is invoked for manifestation and creative inspiration.

5th Mother Teresa's Day. Born in Albania, Agnes Gonxhe Bojaxhiu was seen as the embodiment of a living saint, working in the slums of Calcutta, India, amidst poverty and disease. She was beatified in 1997.

7th Healer's Day. A time to honour healers, learn healing methods and do healing rituals. In Greece, this was the start of the **Eleusinian Mysteries**, a series of initiation ceremonies where the grain and fertility goddess Demeter and her daughter Persephone were honoured.

8th Blessed Virgin Mary's Day. The feast of the nativity of Mary is celebrated in the Orthodox, Anglican and Roman Catholic churches. Revered as the mother of Jesus Christ, Mary is also celebrated in her own right as a symbol of goodness and love. It's also the **Fiestas de Santa Fe**, which has been celebrated in New Mexico since 1712 and features a pet parade, dancing, religious observances, ethnic foods, fireworks and the burning of an effigy of Zozobra, Old Man Gloom.

9th Kiku no Sekku. One of the sacred festivals of Japan, Kiku no Sekku, Chrysanthemum Day, started in the year 910, when the Imperial Court declared the chrysanthemum the national flower.

11th Enkutatash. The Ethiopian new year falls on the 1st day of the month of Meskerem. Enkutatash, which means gift of jewels, marks the end of the rainy season and the blossoming of spring, and was the day the Queen of Sheba returned home after her visit to King Solomon.

13th Egyptian Day of the Dead. An ancient fire festival to honour the deceased and their spirits as they entered the next world, and to revere the goddess Nephthys. It's also **International Chocolate Day**.

19th The Fast of Thoth. This day was dedicated to the Egyptian god Thoth. It fell six weeks after his festival, balancing the earlier celebrations with a full day of praying, meditation and fasting.

21st International Day of Peace. This global event highlights efforts to end conflict, encourage ceasefires and promote peace. It's also **World Gratitude Day**, in which people express appreciation to others.

22nd Ostara. In the southern hemisphere the spring equinox, celebrated by pagans as Ostara, falls around this date, while in the north it's the autumn equinox, **Mabon**. It's also **Hobbit Day**, celebrated by fans of author JRR Tolkein and his *Lord of the Rings* books.

23rd Autumnal Equinox Day. The Shinto festival of **Shubun no Hi** is the middle day of a seven-day period known as Higan, which is a national holiday. People visit the graves of their ancestors to pay their respects, weed the family tombs and leave flowers, incense and food for them, as well as pondering their spiritual beliefs and commitment.

27th Saint Vincent de Paul's Day. Born in France to a peasant family in 1581, he devoted his life to helping the poor. Vincent became a priest, and spent a lot of his time convincing the rich that they should contribute to his charities. His work lives on to this day in the international welfare organisation named after him.

28th Confucius's Day. The birthday of China's most famous philosopher is celebrated on this day in the west and in Taiwan, where it's referred to as Teacher's Day because he is considered the greatest teacher in Chinese history. In China his birthday falls on the 27th day of the eighth lunar month, in late September or October.

29th Saint Michael's Day. It's the feast day of Michael the Archangel, prince of light and patron saint of chivalry, soldiers and warriors. In Celtic lands it's Michaelmas, which marked the end of the harvest and was one of the quarter days when accounts were settled. It's the third quarter day, following Lady Day and Saint John the Baptist's Day.

30th Ivy Month begins. Ivy people are unique, independent and colourful, with their own style and beliefs. They are artistic, talented and often radical thinkers, with a keen intellect and determination and stamina, like ivy, to beat the odds and cling on tenaciously. They are ruthless and shrewd with their finances yet very generous, a good combination, and are compassionate and quick to lend a hand.

◊ In China, the **Mid-Autumn Moon Festival**, known as Chung Chiu or the Mooncake Festival, is second only to New Year's in importance. It falls on the 15th day of the eighth lunar month, often in September. It marks the end of the first harvest, and is a celebration of the moon's association with fertility and femininity, honoured with feasting, festivities, fire dragon dancing, lanterns and mooncakes, which symbolise family unity and perfection. These delicacies are embossed with the characters for longevity and harmony or harvest images.

◊ The Hindu harvest festival of **Onam** is celebrated in India in honour of Mahabali, the mythical Asura king of ancient Kerala. It falls in late August or September. As well as celebrating the harvest, people visit the temples, have family get-togethers, exchange gifts and enjoy dancing and other festivities. It's a time of abundance and plenty.

◊ In the northern hemisphere, the full moon closest to the autumn equinox is the **Harvest Moon**. It is the brightest and most golden of the year, allowing farmers to work through the night to bring the harvest in, and appears to be the biggest. In Japan, there are Harvest Moon viewing events, **Otsukimi**. Historically, nobles gathered to feast as they gazed at the moon and created poems in its honour. Today tables are set with rice cakes and vegies in gratitude for the harvest. In Vietnam, this moon brings **Tet Trung Thu**, an autumn festival where children parade through the streets with lanterns, mooncakes are made and parties held after the hard work of bringing in the harvest.

◊ A popular Hindu festival is **Ganesha Chaturthi**, the birthday of Lord Ganesha, the elephant-headed god of power and wisdom. It falls four days after the new moon in the month of Bhadrapada, in late August or September. New statues of the god are made, a ritual bath is taken, then devotees go to the temple to pray and offer coconuts and sweets.

◊ **Rosh Hashanah**, which means head of the year, is the Jewish new year. It falls on the first day of Tishrei, the seventh month of the Hebrew calendar, usually in September. It is known as the Day of Judgement, the Day of Remembrance and the Day of the Blowing of the Shofar, named after the tradition of blowing this trumpet made from a ram's horn. Prayers are also said and special foods are eaten.

 October

This month was named from the word octo, meaning eight, as it was originally the eighth month of the Roman calendar. In 1582, Pope Gregory XIII made a few adjustments to the leap year rule of the Julian calendar to realign it to the seasons, creating the Gregorian calendar that is used today. To adjust to the new method, 10 days had to be lost, which took place in October 1582. Saint Teresa of Avila, who died on October 4, 1582, was buried the next day – on October 15. **October's flower:** The marigold, which represents health, patience and auspiciousness. Christians called it Mary's Gold and placed it around statues of the Virgin. **Birthstones:** Opal, a symbol of hope, purity and love, referred to as the queen of gems as it embodies the colours of all precious stones, and tourmaline, which helps release emotional blockages and promotes tranquillity and peace.

1st Saint Therese de Lisieux's Day. This nun, who died in 1897 aged 24, is known for her spiritual memoir, *Story of a Soul*. She is recognised as a Doctor of the Church, one of only three women to be so honoured, and canonised as a saint. Known as the Little Flower of Jesus, she's the patron of illness, missions, people with AIDS and florists.

2nd Guiding Spirits Day. Magical practitioners light a candle or a log fire to guide the spirits of the dead back to their home on this day, and give thanks to their spirit guides and guardians for assistance in spiritual development. It's also **Memorial Day for Guardian Angels**, and the Indian national holiday of **Gandhi Jayanti**, which marks the 1869 birthday of Hindu political and spiritual leader Mahatma Gandhi with prayer services, tributes and avoidance of meat and alcohol.

3rd Festival of the Opening of Heaven. Also known as Foundation Day, this South Korean holiday marks the founding of Gojoseon, the kingdom of Korea, in 2333BCE by the god of heaven's grandson.

4th Saint Francis of Assisi's Day. This 13th century friar was born into wealth, but founded the Franciscan Order which embraced poverty and humility. He was a nature lover, and is patron of animals and the environment. It's also **National Cinnamon Bun Day** in Sweden.

9th Felicitas's Day. A day in honour of the Ancient Roman goddess of good fortune, who personified success, prosperity and luck.

11th Meditrinalia. In Ancient Rome, this festival day was celebrated in honour of the goddess of healing, health, longevity and wine.

15th Saint Teresa of Avila's Day. A Spanish mystic and Carmelite nun, she embraced poverty and inflicted torture on herself. She also wrote books, one of which forms the basis of a Caroline Myss release. It's also sacred to **Mars**, Roman god of war, fertility and agriculture.

16th World Food Day. The UN declared this international day to raise awareness about the 850 million people around the world who are starving, primarily in developing nations. And on the 17th it's the UN-declared **Eradication of Poverty Day**, with a similar message.

18th Cernunnos's Day. Sacred to the pagan god of the forest, the hunt, wild animals and fertility. He was a horned god, associated with horned male animals such as stags, and erroneously with the devil. He reflects the seasons of the year and the cycle of life, death and rebirth, and is considered guardian of the forests and its wisdom.

19th Mother Teresa's Day. While her feast day is September 5, the day of her "birthday into heaven", this is the day Albanians celebrate their favourite daughter, a nun, humanitarian and Nobel laureate.

20th Birth of the Bab. A Bahai holy day marking the birth of their spiritual founder, the herald of the Bahai faith, on this day in 1819.

22nd Kurama Himatsuri. This Japanese fire festival illuminates a path for the spirits of the dead, and provides an opportunity for prayer and reverence at the shrines. Boys carrying lit torches make their way to the temples, followed by men wielding larger ones. In Kyoto it's also the **Jidai Matsuri Festival**, a fascinating procession featuring people in elaborate costumes representing the imperial history of Japan.

26th Pasdernik, Day of the Ancients. A traditional Slavic celebration which was a day of remembrance, both for those who had fallen in war and the ancient ones who had guided their ancestors long ago.

28th Reed Month begins. Reed people are vibrant, passionate, decisive and forceful. They can be impatient at times, but simply want to achieve quickly, and they have a strong code of honour. They are secret keepers, delving through layers of meaning to understand the truth and hidden wisdom, and can coax information from people. They are sometimes perceived as arrogant, because they dislike weakness. They are well respected and have a powerful presence.

30th Devil's Night. Also known as Mischief Night, this event takes place on the eve of Halloween, when people in the US play practical jokes, such as egging houses, on people in their neighbourhood.

31st Halloween. This night of fun and frivolity sees children dressing up as witches, ghosts and other spooky creatures, and going trick or treating. It's based on the old Celtic festival of **Samhain**, which falls around this day in the northern hemisphere, while in the southern hemisphere many pagans celebrate **Beltane** at this time of year.

◊ In North America, the October full moon is known as the **Hunter's Moon**, as it has an eerie glow and travels low across the sky, illuminating the night better than some other full moons, and making it easier to hunt nocturnal animals. The Feast of the Hunter's Moon is celebrated with dancing, drumming, storytelling and revelry.

◊ In India, Diwali, the five-day **Festival of Lights**, begins on the new moon that falls between October 13 and November 14. It's the biggest festival in India, celebrated by Hindus, Buddhists, Sikhs and others all around the world. Lanterns are lit to ward off evil spirits, oil lamps burn to signify the victory of light over dark within each person, firecrackers explode into sprays of light, gifts are exchanged and garlands are made from marigold flowers and mango leaves.

◊ **Yom Kippur** is the final day of the Ten Days of Repentance that began with Rosh Hashanah. Also known as the Day of Atonement, it's the most solemn Jewish holy day, focusing on repentance. People fast and pray for 25 hours, trying to atone for their sins. Five days later is Sukkoth, the **Feast of the Tabernacles**, which commemorates the 40 years the Israelites spent walking in the wilderness.

◊ In Canada, **Thanksgiving Day**, Jour d'action de Grace, falls on the second Monday in October. It's a festival of gratitude for the harvest and the blessings of the prior year, and a time of family gatherings.

◊ **Navaratri** is a nine-night Hindu festival that marks the beginning of winter. It is a celebration of the divine feminine, where nine forms of the universal mother, known as Durga, are worshipped. She is also known as Devi (goddess) and Shakti (energy and power), and is celebrated with dance, song, offerings and other rituals. The **Durga Puja** is a Bengali festival that also involves worship of the goddess Durga, and is celebrated in many places in the east, including India, Kashmir, Bengal and Nepal, in September or October. On the full moon following Durga Puja, the goddess **Lakshmi** is honoured when she returns to earth to bless people with abundance for the year ahead.

◊ The Islamic month of fasting, **Ramadan**, ends on the first day of the 10th month of the lunar calendar, with the festival of **Eid ul-Fitr**, with prayer ceremonies, family visits, a ritual breakfast and celebration.

November

November is the 11th month, but it gets its name from novem, the Latin word for nine, as it was originally the ninth month of the Roman calendar. It's one of only four months with 30 days, and starts on the same day of the week as March and, in non-leap years, February. **November's flower:** Chrysanthemums, associated with friendship, compassion and happiness. **Birthstone:** Topaz, which signifies friendship and provides strength, motivation and optimism.

1st All Saints Day. This day honours all the saints, while the following, All Souls Day, is for the souls of departed loved ones. In Latin America it's **el Dia de los Muertos**, the Day of the Dead, when people pray for and remember friends and family members who have died. Altars are built in the home to honour them, decorated with sugar skulls and marigolds, graves are visited and there are festivals and parades.

3rd Culture Day. In Japan, this was once celebrated as the anniversary of Emperor Meiji's birth, but when the constitution was signed on this day in 1946 it was changed to commemorate local culture and identity, promote peace and freedom and celebrate Japanese achievement.

4th Plebian Games. In Ancient Rome, this two-week festival was held in honour of Jupiter, the king of the gods and the deity of sky, thunder and law. There were sporting contests, drama performances, singing and dancing, culminating with a huge banquet on the 13th, Epulum Jovis, a celebration of thanks to Jupiter for the abundant harvest.

5th Guy Fawkes's Night. A night of fireworks, bonfires and parties to commemorate the foiling of the Gunpowder Plot of 1605, when Guy Fawkes and his friends planned to blow up the English Houses of Parliament and kill King James I to install a Catholic monarch.

8th Archangelovden. Archangel's Day in Bulgaria honours Archangel Michael with a ceremonial meal, an animal sacrifice and prayers in the hope that he will help people through the harshness of winter.

9th Schicksalstag. In Germany this day, meaning day of fate, is the anniversary of several momentous events, from the execution of liberal leader Robert Blum in 1848 to the end of the monarchy and the country's transformation to a republic in 1918; the Beerhall coup d'etat that marked the emergence of the Nazi Party in 1923; Kristallnacht, an anti-Jewish pogrom, in 1938; and the fall of the Berlin Wall in 1989.

10th Saint Martin's Eve. This saint, a fourth century Roman soldier turned monk, is celebrated with feasting, wine tasting, gifts for the children and a procession. Traditionally this night was the last meal before 40 days of fasting, so everyone ate well before observing the restrictions that started on Saint Martin's Day, known as Matinmas.

11th Remembrance Day. Also known as Veterans Day in some countries, and Armistice Day in others, this commemoration of the end of World War I has become a day to remember all those who have died in war, and is symbolised by the wearing of red poppies.

14th Children's Day. While the international celebration in honour of kids takes place on the 20th, the anniversary of the 1959 signing of the Declaration of the Rights of the Child, in India it falls on the birthday of Jawaharlal Nehru, the country's first prime minister, who was committed to protecting children. It's also **Feast of the Musicians**, a Celtic holiday still observed by some, where bards and other druids composed and performed songs celebrating the magic of the earth.

16th Hecate's Night. This was the night people believed the Greek goddess of the crossroads and the wilderness roamed the earth with her hounds, and it became a time of initiations into the Mysteries.

19th International Men's Day. An international event that focuses on men's health and wellbeing, improving gender relations, promoting gender equality and highlighting positive male role models.

22nd Saint Cecilia's Day. An Italian noblewoman who took a vow of chastity, she was martyred in the third century, along with her husband and brother-in-law. She is the patron saint of musicians.

25th Elder Month begins. Elder tree people are powerful, persuasive and willing to challenge injustice. They are impulsive, curious and at times restless, with a love of freedom and adventure. They have a great thirst for knowledge and honesty, which can be brutal, with a philosophical, deeply thoughtful bent. Many are talented in music and art or are great healers, and are very considerate of others. They are meditative, and grow and change a lot throughout their lifetime. It's also the feast day of **Saint Catherine**, patron of philosophers, who is believed to be a Christianised version of Nemesis, the goddess of fate and destiny for whom the great spinning fire wheels, later called Catherine Wheels, were rolled down hills as part of pagan fire festivals.

25th International Day for the Elimination of Violence Against Women. The UN General Assembly designated this day to raise public awareness of the issue around the world. The date commemorates the 1960 assassination of the three Mirabal sisters, political activists in the Dominican Republic, on the orders of the country's ruler.

27th Sophia's Day. A celebration in honour of the Greek goddess of inner truth, knowledge and justice, who was the personification of wisdom and considered to be the beginning of all the things.

30th Saint Andrew's Day. Andrew was a fisherman and follower of John the Baptist, and the first disciple of Jesus. He became a missionary, and was crucified in Greece circa 70CE. He was the younger brother of Simon, who became Saint Peter, and is the patron saint of Scotland, Russia, Sicily and Greece, as well as of fishermen. In Scotland this is their national day. It's also a day sacred to **Hecate**, the goddess of the crossroads, the three paths, sorcery and lunar phases. Offerings of honeycakes and mushrooms are still left out for her in Greece, and modern witches revere her as a triple goddess of wisdom and change.

◊ The fourth Thursday in November is **Thanksgiving Day** in the US, a harvest festival that can be traced back to 1620, when early settlers aboard the Mayflower landed in the wrong spot and would have perished but for the assistance of the Native Americans who lived there. It remains a day of family get-togethers and giving thanks.

◊ In November in Japan, **Autumn Foliage**, Momiji, is the period when temperatures fall to 10°C and the leaves explode in vibrant colours. Momiji-gari – autumn-foliage viewing – is popular across the country, with people going into the mountains to observe nature's beauty.

◊ It's also **Novel Writing Month**, an international event where budding authors vow to finish (and upload) a 50,000 word novel in 30 days, focusing on quality not quantity. They can edit later; the intent is to start a book and get procrastinators over the hurdle of a blank page.

◊ And it's the time of **Movember**, a month-long charity event to raise awareness and funds for men's health issues, such as prostate cancer and depression, by men being sponsored to grow a mo. It began in Australia and New Zealand but has expanded to Canada, Spain, the UK and US. The name combines the words Moustache and November.

◊ The fourth Sunday before Christmas is **Advent Sunday**, the beginning of Advent, a period of preparation, special lessons and waiting for Jesus's birthday, which marks the start of the western liturgical year. The advent calendars that count down to Christmas, which are now more synonymous with chocolate, grew out of this tradition.

December

The last month of the Gregorian year gets its name from decem, the Latin word for 10, as it was originally the 10th month of the Roman calendar. It is the time of the Cold Moon, known as frosty month or month of winter in many European countries. **December's flowers:** Narcissus, one of the few blooms to brave the winter snow in northern climes, which represent sweetness and purity, along with poinsettias and holly. **Birthstone:** Turquoise, which boosts psychic abilities, protects from negativity and signifies love and compassion.

1st Poseidon's Day. A festival dedicated to Poseidon, the Greek god of the sea and of rebirth, whose Roman counterpart was Neptune.

3rd Rhea's Day. A day sacred to the Greek goddess who represented Gaia, the deified earth. She was the queen of heaven and the mother of the gods, and oversaw fertility, motherhood and regeneration.

5th International Volunteers Day. Established by the UN in 1985, this day honours all the people who volunteer for a good cause, and highlights the important role they play in their communities.

6th Saint Nicholas's Day. Nicholas was a fourth century bishop from Turkey, who threw a bag of gold coins down a chimney to save a girl from prostitution, where they landed in her stockings. He became the model for Santa Claus, from the German Sankt Niklaus. The day is also dedicated to **Odin**, the Norse god of war, death and wisdom.

8th Feast of the Immaculate Conception. Although this marks the day the Virgin Mary was conceived, it also celebrates the immaculate conception of Jesus. And it's **Bodhi Day**, marking the date that the Buddha sat under the Bodhi tree and found enlightenment.

10th Human Rights Day. The UN adopted the Universal Declaration of Human Rights on this day in 1948, and celebrates with political conferences and cultural events highlighting human rights issues. It is also **Lux Mundi**, a Roman festival still celebrated in Europe, which translates as light of the world, and a day sacred to **Libertas**, goddess of freedom, liberty and light who remains the burning torch of hope.

11th Arianrhod's Day. The Celtic mother goddess associated with fertility and the moon is honoured on this day as ruler of the wheel of the heavens. It's also dedicated to **Bruma**, Roman goddess of winter.

12th Dia de Nuestra Senora de Guadalupe. Our Lady of Guadalupe commemorates the date in 1531 that Mary appeared to a Mexican boy. It's a national fiesta with a mass, traditional music, dancing and gifts. Some pilgrims walk on their knees on the stones to the church.

16th Boston Tea Party. On this day in 1773, people in Boston, USA, fed up with the British Tea Act that forced them to buy overtaxed tea, protested against the colonial power, throwing the tea into Boston Harbor, a key event in the lead up to the American Revolution. In Latin American countries, the nine-day **Las Posadas** festival begins, symbolising Mary's attempt to find somewhere to give birth. It was begun by a priest who wanted to replace the celebration of the birth of the Aztec sun god. It's also the **Day of Reconciliation**, a public holiday in South Africa that fosters reconciliation between racial groups.

17th Saturnalia. In Ancient Rome, this festival in honour of the harvest god Saturn, and the upcoming winter solstice, was a time of merrymaking and fun. For a week there was a ban on business and war, and people partied in the streets and treated each other as equals.

20th Ceridwen's Day. A day sacred to the Celtic goddess of fertility, life and death. She is the keeper of the cauldron of transformation, knowledge and rebirth, with its healing powers and ability to inspire.

21st Solstice. Around this day in the southern hemisphere is the summer solstice, the longest day and shortest night of the year, known as **Litha**, while in the northern hemisphere it is the winter solstice, the longest night, and several winter celebrations such as **Yule**.

23rd Karachun. An old pagan solstice festival of Slavic origin, it celebrated the time dark spirits were most powerful. On this night the old sun god, Hors, was defeated by the black god, but two days later he was resurrected and transformed into Koleda, the new sun god.

24th Birch Month begins. Birch tree people are imaginative, vivacious and determined, focusing on career and quite private in their personal life. They have great personal potential, but must be persistent to achieve it. They are emotional, friendly, unpretentious and calm, and they make great friends, although it can take time to get close to them. Birch starts the Celtic tree calendar, and thus these people have the energies associated with new beginnings. It's also **Christmas Eve**.

25th Christmas Day. Marking the birthday of Jesus in Bethlehem, this is a religious holiday around the world, as well as a more secular, some would say commercial, festival that brings families together.

It's the fourth of the Christian quarter days. It is also **Newtonmas**, which celebrates science and marks the birthday of Isaac Newton with a tree decorated with apples and the giving of educational gifts.

26th Kwanzaa. A week-long festival with its roots in the 1960s black nationalist movement, it aims to help African Americans reconnect with their cultural heritage. There are candle-lighting rituals, feasts and gift giving. It's also **Saint Stephen's Day**, in honour of a first century church deacon who was martyred, and **Boxing Day**, a public holiday when donations for tradesmen were traditionally collected.

27th Saint John's Day. It's the feast day of Saint John, known as the Apostle and Evangelist, and credited with writing some of *The Bible*. It's also the birthday of **Freya**, the Norse goddess of love, beauty and fertility, who led the Valkyries, and for whom Friday is named.

31st New Year's Eve. A time of celebration, reflection and resolutions for the coming year. In Scotland, the three-day festival of **Hogmanay** begins, with fireball swinging, poi, pipe bands, drumming and fireworks. In Japan, temples ring their bells 108 times, known as **joya-no-kane**, to rid humans of the 108 earthly desires that lead to suffering.

◊ On the 10th day of Dhul Hijja, in November or December, Muslims celebrate Eid ul-Adha, the **Festival of Sacrifice**, to commemorate the willingness of Abraham to sacrifice his son to prove his obedience to God. There are prayers, sermons, sacrifices and donations to the poor.

◊ The eight-day Jewish festival of **Chanukkah**, the Festival of Lights, starts on the 25th day of Kislev, which usually begins in December. Candles are lit in the menorah, a special candelabra, to commemorate historical events. Although it has become known as the Jewish Christmas, Chanukkah had its roots in a revolt against assimilation.

◊ On the winter solstice in Japan, the Shinto festival **Tohji-Taisai** honours the sun goddess Amaterasu and marks the end of the yin period of the sun, when it's declining in strength, and the start of its yang period. Long ago Amaterasu withdrew into a cave, angry at the chaos her brother unleashed, and had to be lured out with music, dance and raucous revelry – which is repeated today to ensure she shines.

◊ In China, the winter solstice is **Dongzhi**, winter's extreme. It's a time of temple ceremonies and family get-togethers, with the making and eating of tangyuan, rice balls that symbolise reunion. The day encapsulates yin and yang, universal balance. From this day forward there'll be more daylight, and an increase in positive energy flowing in.

2009 and 2015

JANUARY
M	T	W	T	F	S	S
			01	02	03	04
05	06	07	08	09	10	11
12	13	14	15	16	17	18
19	20	21	22	23	24	25
26	27	28	29	30	31	

FEBRUARY
M	T	W	T	F	S	S
						01
02	03	04	05	06	07	08
09	10	11	12	13	14	15
16	17	18	19	20	21	22
23	24	25	26	27	28	

MARCH
M	T	W	T	F	S	S
						01
02	03	04	05	06	07	08
09	10	11	12	13	14	15
16	17	18	19	20	21	22
23	24	25	26	27	28	29
30	31					

APRIL
M	T	W	T	F	S	S
		01	02	03	04	05
06	07	08	09	10	11	12
13	14	15	16	17	18	19
20	21	22	23	24	25	26
27	28	29	30			

MAY
M	T	W	T	F	S	S
				01	02	03
04	05	06	07	08	09	10
11	12	13	14	15	16	17
18	19	20	21	22	23	24
25	26	27	28	29	30	31

JUNE
M	T	W	T	F	S	S
01	02	03	04	05	06	07
08	09	10	11	12	13	14
15	16	17	18	19	20	21
22	23	24	25	26	27	28
29	30					

JULY
M	T	W	T	F	S	S
		01	02	03	04	05
06	07	08	09	10	11	12
13	14	15	16	17	18	19
20	21	22	23	24	25	26
27	28	29	30	31		

AUGUST
M	T	W	T	F	S	S
					01	02
03	04	05	06	07	08	09
10	11	12	13	14	15	16
17	18	19	20	21	22	23
24	25	26	27	28	29	30
31						

SEPTEMBER
M	T	W	T	F	S	S
	01	02	03	04	05	06
07	08	09	10	11	12	13
14	15	16	17	18	19	20
21	22	23	24	25	26	27
28	29	30				

OCTOBER
M	T	W	T	F	S	S
			01	02	03	04
05	06	07	08	09	10	11
12	13	14	15	16	17	18
19	20	21	22	23	24	25
26	27	28	29	30	31	

NOVEMBER
M	T	W	T	F	S	S
						01
02	03	04	05	06	07	08
09	10	11	12	13	14	15
16	17	18	19	20	21	22
23	24	25	26	27	28	29
30						

DECEMBER
M	T	W	T	F	S	S
	01	02	03	04	05	06
07	08	09	10	11	12	13
14	15	16	17	18	19	20
21	22	23	24	25	26	27
28	29	30	31			

2010

JANUARY
M	T	W	T	F	S	S
				01	02	03
04	05	06	07	08	09	10
11	12	13	14	15	16	17
18	19	20	21	22	23	24
25	26	27	28	29	30	31

FEBRUARY
M	T	W	T	F	S	S
01	02	03	04	05	06	07
08	09	10	11	12	13	14
15	16	17	18	19	20	21
22	23	24	25	26	27	28

MARCH
M	T	W	T	F	S	S
01	02	03	04	05	06	07
08	09	10	11	12	13	14
15	16	17	18	19	20	21
22	23	24	25	26	27	28
29	30	31				

APRIL
M	T	W	T	F	S	S
			01	02	03	04
05	06	07	08	09	10	11
12	13	14	15	16	17	18
19	20	21	22	23	24	25
26	27	28	29	30		

MAY
M	T	W	T	F	S	S
					01	02
03	04	05	06	07	08	09
10	11	12	13	14	15	16
17	18	19	20	21	22	23
24	25	26	27	28	29	30
31						

JUNE
M	T	W	T	F	S	S
	01	02	03	04	05	06
07	08	09	10	11	12	13
14	15	16	17	18	19	20
21	22	23	24	25	26	27
28	29	30				

JULY
M	T	W	T	F	S	S
			01	02	03	04
05	06	07	08	09	10	11
12	13	14	15	16	17	18
19	20	21	22	23	24	25
26	27	28	29	30	31	

AUGUST
M	T	W	T	F	S	S
						01
02	03	04	05	06	07	08
09	10	11	12	13	14	15
16	17	18	19	20	21	22
23	24	25	26	27	28	29
30	31					

SEPTEMBER
M	T	W	T	F	S	S
		01	02	03	04	05
06	07	08	09	10	11	12
13	14	15	16	17	18	19
20	21	22	23	24	25	26
27	28	29	30			

OCTOBER
M	T	W	T	F	S	S
				01	02	03
04	05	06	07	08	09	10
11	12	13	14	15	16	17
18	19	20	21	22	23	24
25	26	27	28	29	30	31

NOVEMBER
M	T	W	T	F	S	S
01	02	03	04	05	06	07
08	09	10	11	12	13	14
15	16	17	18	19	20	21
22	23	24	25	26	27	28
29	30					

DECEMBER
M	T	W	T	F	S	S
		01	02	03	04	05
06	07	08	09	10	11	12
13	14	15	16	17	18	19
20	21	22	23	24	25	26
27	28	29	30	31		

2011

JANUARY
M	T	W	T	F	S	S
31					01	02
03	04	05	06	07	08	09
10	11	12	13	14	15	16
17	18	19	20	21	22	23
24	25	26	27	28	29	30

FEBRUARY
M	T	W	T	F	S	S
	01	02	03	04	05	06
07	08	09	10	11	12	13
14	15	16	17	18	19	20
21	22	23	24	25	26	27
28						

MARCH
M	T	W	T	F	S	S
	01	02	03	04	05	06
07	08	09	10	11	12	13
14	15	16	17	18	19	20
21	22	23	24	25	26	27
28	29	30	31			

APRIL
M	T	W	T	F	S	S
				01	02	03
04	05	06	07	08	09	10
11	12	13	14	15	16	17
18	19	20	21	22	23	24
25	26	27	28	29	30	

MAY
M	T	W	T	F	S	S
30	31					01
02	03	04	05	06	07	08
09	10	11	12	13	14	15
16	17	18	19	20	21	22
23	24	25	26	27	28	29

JUNE
M	T	W	T	F	S	S
		01	02	03	04	05
06	07	08	09	10	11	12
13	14	15	16	17	18	19
20	21	22	23	24	25	26
27	28	29	30			

JULY
M	T	W	T	F	S	S
				01	02	03
04	05	06	07	08	09	10
11	12	13	14	15	16	17
18	19	20	21	22	23	24
25	26	27	28	29	30	31

AUGUST
M	T	W	T	F	S	S
01	02	03	04	05	06	07
08	09	10	11	12	13	14
15	16	17	18	19	20	21
22	23	24	25	26	27	28
29	30	31				

SEPTEMBER
M	T	W	T	F	S	S
			01	02	03	04
05	06	07	08	09	10	11
12	13	14	15	16	17	18
19	20	21	22	23	24	25
26	27	28	29	30		

OCTOBER
M	T	W	T	F	S	S
31					01	02
03	04	05	06	07	08	09
10	11	12	13	14	15	16
17	18	19	20	21	22	23
24	25	26	27	28	29	30

NOVEMBER
M	T	W	T	F	S	S
	01	02	03	04	05	06
07	08	09	10	11	12	13
14	15	16	17	18	19	20
21	22	23	24	25	26	27
28	29	30				

DECEMBER
M	T	W	T	F	S	S
			01	02	03	04
05	06	07	08	09	10	11
12	13	14	15	16	17	18
19	20	21	22	23	24	25
26	27	28	29	30	31	

11-Year Calendar ◊ 97

2012

JANUARY
M	T	W	T	F	S	S
30	31					01
02	03	04	05	06	07	08
09	10	11	12	13	14	15
16	17	18	19	20	21	22
23	24	25	26	27	28	29

FEBRUARY
M	T	W	T	F	S	S
		01	02	03	04	05
06	07	08	09	10	11	12
13	14	15	16	17	18	19
20	21	22	23	24	25	26
27	28	29				

MARCH
M	T	W	T	F	S	S
			01	02	03	04
05	06	07	08	09	10	11
12	13	14	15	16	17	18
19	20	21	22	23	24	25
26	27	28	29	30	31	

APRIL
M	T	W	T	F	S	S
						01
02	03	04	05	06	07	08
09	10	11	12	13	14	15
16	17	18	19	20	21	22
23	24	25	26	27	28	29
30						

MAY
M	T	W	T	F	S	S
	01	02	03	04	05	06
07	08	09	10	11	12	13
14	15	16	17	18	19	20
21	22	23	24	25	26	27
28	29	30	31			

JUNE
M	T	W	T	F	S	S
				01	02	03
04	05	06	07	08	09	10
11	12	13	14	15	16	17
18	19	20	21	22	23	24
25	26	27	28	29	30	

JULY
M	T	W	T	F	S	S
30	31					01
02	03	04	05	06	07	08
09	10	11	12	13	14	15
16	17	18	19	20	21	22
23	24	25	26	27	28	29

AUGUST
M	T	W	T	F	S	S
		01	02	03	04	05
06	07	08	09	10	11	12
13	14	15	16	17	18	19
20	21	22	23	24	25	26
27	28	29	30	31		

SEPTEMBER
M	T	W	T	F	S	S
					01	02
03	04	05	06	07	08	09
10	11	12	13	14	15	16
17	18	19	20	21	22	23
24	25	26	27	28	29	30

OCTOBER
M	T	W	T	F	S	S
01	02	03	04	05	06	07
08	09	10	11	12	13	14
15	16	17	18	19	20	21
22	23	24	25	26	27	28
29	30	31				

NOVEMBER
M	T	W	T	F	S	S
			01	02	03	04
05	06	07	08	09	10	11
12	13	14	15	16	17	18
19	20	21	22	23	24	25
26	27	28	29	30		

DECEMBER
M	T	W	T	F	S	S
31					01	02
03	04	05	06	07	08	09
10	11	12	13	14	15	16
17	18	19	20	21	22	23
24	25	26	27	28	29	30

2013 and 2019

JANUARY
M	T	W	T	F	S	S
	01	02	03	04	05	06
07	08	09	10	11	12	13
14	15	16	17	18	19	20
21	22	23	24	25	26	27
28	29	30	31			

FEBRUARY
M	T	W	T	F	S	S
				01	02	03
04	05	06	07	08	09	10
11	12	13	14	15	16	17
18	19	20	21	22	23	24
25	26	27	28			

MARCH
M	T	W	T	F	S	S
				01	02	03
04	05	06	07	08	09	10
11	12	13	14	15	16	17
18	19	20	21	22	23	24
25	26	27	28	29	30	31

APRIL
M	T	W	T	F	S	S
01	02	03	04	05	06	07
08	09	10	11	12	13	14
15	16	17	18	19	20	21
22	23	24	25	26	27	28
29	30					

MAY
M	T	W	T	F	S	S
		01	02	03	04	05
06	07	08	09	10	11	12
13	14	15	16	17	18	19
20	21	22	23	24	25	26
27	28	29	30	31		

JUNE
M	T	W	T	F	S	S
					01	02
03	04	05	06	07	08	09
10	11	12	13	14	15	16
17	18	19	20	21	22	23
24	25	26	27	28	29	30

JULY
M	T	W	T	F	S	S
01	02	03	04	05	06	07
08	09	10	11	12	13	14
15	16	17	18	19	20	21
22	23	24	25	26	27	28
29	30	31				

AUGUST
M	T	W	T	F	S	S
			01	02	03	04
05	06	07	08	09	10	11
12	13	14	15	16	17	18
19	20	21	22	23	24	25
26	27	28	29	30	31	

SEPTEMBER
M	T	W	T	F	S	S
30						01
02	03	04	05	06	07	08
09	10	11	12	13	14	15
16	17	18	19	20	21	22
23	24	25	26	27	28	29

OCTOBER
M	T	W	T	F	S	S
	01	02	03	04	05	06
07	08	09	10	11	12	13
14	15	16	17	18	19	20
21	22	23	24	25	26	27
28	29	30	31			

NOVEMBER
M	T	W	T	F	S	S
				01	02	03
04	05	06	07	08	09	10
11	12	13	14	15	16	17
18	19	20	21	22	23	24
25	26	27	28	29	30	

DECEMBER
M	T	W	T	F	S	S
30	31					01
02	03	04	05	06	07	08
09	10	11	12	13	14	15
16	17	18	19	20	21	22
23	24	25	26	27	28	29

2014

JANUARY
M	T	W	T	F	S	S
		01	02	03	04	05
06	07	08	09	10	11	12
13	14	15	16	17	18	19
20	21	22	23	24	25	26
27	28	29	30	31		

FEBRUARY
M	T	W	T	F	S	S
					01	02
03	04	05	06	07	08	09
10	11	12	13	14	15	16
17	18	19	20	21	22	23
24	25	26	27	28		

MARCH
M	T	W	T	F	S	S
31					01	02
03	04	05	06	07	08	09
10	11	12	13	14	15	16
17	18	19	20	21	22	23
24	25	26	27	28	29	30

APRIL
M	T	W	T	F	S	S
	01	02	03	04	05	06
07	08	09	10	11	12	13
14	15	16	17	18	19	20
21	22	23	24	25	26	27
28	29	30				

MAY
M	T	W	T	F	S	S
			01	02	03	04
05	06	07	08	09	10	11
12	13	14	15	16	17	18
19	20	21	22	23	24	25
26	27	28	29	30	31	

JUNE
M	T	W	T	F	S	S
30						01
02	03	04	05	06	07	08
09	10	11	12	13	14	15
16	17	18	19	20	21	22
23	24	25	26	27	28	29

JULY
M	T	W	T	F	S	S
	01	02	03	04	05	06
07	08	09	10	11	12	13
14	15	16	17	18	19	20
21	22	23	24	25	26	27
28	29	30	31			

AUGUST
M	T	W	T	F	S	S
				01	02	03
04	05	06	07	08	09	10
11	12	13	14	15	16	17
18	19	20	21	22	23	24
25	26	27	28	29	30	31

SEPTEMBER
M	T	W	T	F	S	S
01	02	03	04	05	06	07
08	09	10	11	12	13	14
15	16	17	18	19	20	21
22	23	24	25	26	27	28
29	30					

OCTOBER
M	T	W	T	F	S	S
		01	02	03	04	05
06	07	08	09	10	11	12
13	14	15	16	17	18	19
20	21	22	23	24	25	26
27	28	29	30	31		

NOVEMBER
M	T	W	T	F	S	S
					01	02
03	04	05	06	07	08	09
10	11	12	13	14	15	16
17	18	19	20	21	22	23
24	25	26	27	28	29	30

DECEMBER
M	T	W	T	F	S	S
01	02	03	04	05	06	07
08	09	10	11	12	13	14
15	16	17	18	19	20	21
22	23	24	25	26	27	28
29	30	31				

2016

JANUARY
M	T	W	T	F	S	S
				01	02	03
04	05	06	07	08	09	10
11	12	13	14	15	16	17
18	19	20	21	22	23	24
25	26	27	28	29	30	31

FEBRUARY
M	T	W	T	F	S	S
01	02	03	04	05	06	07
08	09	10	11	12	13	14
15	16	17	18	19	20	21
22	23	24	25	26	27	28
29						

MARCH
M	T	W	T	F	S	S
	01	02	03	04	05	06
07	08	09	10	11	12	13
14	15	16	17	18	19	20
21	22	23	24	25	26	27
28	29	30	31			

APRIL
M	T	W	T	F	S	S
				01	02	03
04	05	06	07	08	09	10
11	12	13	14	15	16	17
18	19	20	21	22	23	24
25	26	27	28	29	30	

MAY
M	T	W	T	F	S	S
30	31					01
02	03	04	05	06	07	08
09	10	11	12	13	14	15
16	17	18	19	20	21	22
23	24	25	26	27	28	29

JUNE
M	T	W	T	F	S	S
		01	02	03	04	05
06	07	08	09	10	11	12
13	14	15	16	17	18	19
20	21	22	23	24	25	26
27	28	29	30			

JULY
M	T	W	T	F	S	S
				01	02	03
04	05	06	07	08	09	10
11	12	13	14	15	16	17
18	19	20	21	22	23	24
25	26	27	28	29	30	31

AUGUST
M	T	W	T	F	S	S
01	02	03	04	05	06	07
08	09	10	11	12	13	14
15	16	17	18	19	20	21
22	23	24	25	26	27	28
29	30	31				

SEPTEMBER
M	T	W	T	F	S	S
			01	02	03	04
05	06	07	08	09	10	11
12	13	14	15	16	17	18
19	20	21	22	23	24	25
26	27	28	29	30		

OCTOBER
M	T	W	T	F	S	S
					01	02
03	04	05	06	07	08	09
10	11	12	13	14	15	16
17	18	19	20	21	22	23
24	25	26	27	28	29	30
31						

NOVEMBER
M	T	W	T	F	S	S
	01	02	03	04	05	06
07	08	09	10	11	12	13
14	15	16	17	18	19	20
21	22	23	24	25	26	27
28	29	30				

DECEMBER
M	T	W	T	F	S	S
			01	02	03	04
05	06	07	08	09	10	11
12	13	14	15	16	17	18
19	20	21	22	23	24	25
26	27	28	29	30	31	

2017

JANUARY
M	T	W	T	F	S	S
30	31					01
02	03	04	05	06	07	08
09	10	11	12	13	14	15
16	17	18	19	20	21	22
23	24	25	26	27	28	29

FEBRUARY
M	T	W	T	F	S	S
		01	02	03	04	05
06	07	08	09	10	11	12
13	14	15	16	17	18	19
20	21	22	23	24	25	26
27	28					

MARCH
M	T	W	T	F	S	S
		01	02	03	04	05
06	07	08	09	10	11	12
13	14	15	16	17	18	19
20	21	22	23	24	25	26
27	28	29	30	31		

APRIL
M	T	W	T	F	S	S
					01	02
03	04	05	06	07	08	09
10	11	12	13	14	15	16
17	18	19	20	21	22	23
24	25	26	27	28	29	30

MAY
M	T	W	T	F	S	S
01	02	03	04	05	06	07
08	09	10	11	12	13	14
15	16	17	18	19	20	21
22	23	24	25	26	27	28
29	30	31				

JUNE
M	T	W	T	F	S	S
			01	02	03	04
05	06	07	08	09	10	11
12	13	14	15	16	17	18
19	20	21	22	23	24	25
26	27	28	29	30		

JULY
M	T	W	T	F	S	S
31					01	02
03	04	05	06	07	08	09
10	11	12	13	14	15	16
17	18	19	20	21	22	23
24	25	26	27	28	29	30

AUGUST
M	T	W	T	F	S	S
	01	02	03	04	05	06
07	08	09	10	11	12	13
14	15	16	17	18	19	20
21	22	23	24	25	26	27
28	29	30	31			

SEPTEMBER
M	T	W	T	F	S	S
				01	02	03
04	05	06	07	08	09	10
11	12	13	14	15	16	17
18	19	20	21	22	23	24
25	26	27	28	29	30	

OCTOBER
M	T	W	T	F	S	S
30	31					01
02	03	04	05	06	07	08
09	10	11	12	13	14	15
16	17	18	19	20	21	22
23	24	25	26	27	28	29

NOVEMBER
M	T	W	T	F	S	S
		01	02	03	04	05
06	07	08	09	10	11	12
13	14	15	16	17	18	19
20	21	22	23	24	25	26
27	28	29	30			

DECEMBER
M	T	W	T	F	S	S
				01	02	03
04	05	06	07	08	09	10
11	12	13	14	15	16	17
18	19	20	21	22	23	24
25	26	27	28	29	30	31

2018

JANUARY
M	T	W	T	F	S	S
01	02	03	04	05	06	07
08	09	10	11	12	13	14
15	16	17	18	19	20	21
22	23	24	25	26	27	28
29	30	31				

FEBRUARY
M	T	W	T	F	S	S
			01	02	03	04
05	06	07	08	09	10	11
12	13	14	15	16	17	18
19	20	21	22	23	24	25
26	27	28				

MARCH
M	T	W	T	F	S	S
			01	02	03	04
05	06	07	08	09	10	11
12	13	14	15	16	17	18
19	20	21	22	23	24	25
26	27	28	29	30	31	

APRIL
M	T	W	T	F	S	S
30						01
02	03	04	05	06	07	08
09	10	11	12	13	14	15
16	17	18	19	20	21	22
23	24	25	26	27	28	29

MAY
M	T	W	T	F	S	S
	01	02	03	04	05	06
07	08	09	10	11	12	13
14	15	16	17	18	19	20
21	22	23	24	25	26	27
28	29	30	31			

JUNE
M	T	W	T	F	S	S
				01	02	03
04	05	06	07	08	09	10
11	12	13	14	15	16	17
18	19	20	21	22	23	24
25	26	27	28	29	30	

JULY
M	T	W	T	F	S	S
30	31					01
02	03	04	05	06	07	08
09	10	11	12	13	14	15
16	17	18	19	20	21	22
23	24	25	26	27	28	29

AUGUST
M	T	W	T	F	S	S
		01	02	03	04	05
06	07	08	09	10	11	12
13	14	15	16	17	18	19
20	21	22	23	24	25	26
27	28	29	30	31		

SEPTEMBER
M	T	W	T	F	S	S
					01	02
03	04	05	06	07	08	09
10	11	12	13	14	15	16
17	18	19	20	21	22	23
24	25	26	27	28	29	30

OCTOBER
M	T	W	T	F	S	S
01	02	03	04	05	06	07
08	09	10	11	12	13	14
15	16	17	18	19	20	21
22	23	24	25	26	27	28
29	30	31				

NOVEMBER
M	T	W	T	F	S	S
			01	02	03	04
05	06	07	08	09	10	11
12	13	14	15	16	17	18
19	20	21	22	23	24	25
26	27	28	29	30		

DECEMBER
M	T	W	T	F	S	S
31					01	02
03	04	05	06	07	08	09
10	11	12	13	14	15	16
17	18	19	20	21	22	23
24	25	26	27	28	29	30

"Whatever you can do, or dream you can, begin it. Boldness has genius, power and magic in it."
— Goethe, German philosopher

"It is never too late to become what you might have been."
George Eliot, English novelist

"Whether you think you can or think you can't, you are right."
Henry Ford, American businessman

> "I have always been delighted at the prospect of a new day, a fresh try, one more start, with perhaps a bit of magic waiting somewhere behind the morning."
>
> JB Priestley, English author

"Some men see things as they are and say: 'Why?' Others dream of things that never were and say: 'Why not?'"

George Bernard Shaw, Irish playwright

"It's not because things are difficult that we do not dare; it's because we do not dare that they are difficult."

Seneca, first century Roman philosopher

Come to the edge.
"We might fall."
Come to the edge.
"It's too high."
Come to the edge!
And they came.
And he pushed them.
And they flew.

Christopher Logue, UK poet

"*Now and then it's good to pause in our pursuit of happiness and just be happy.*"
Guillaume Apollinaire, French poet

"Life is without meaning. You bring the meaning to it. The meaning of life is whatever you ascribe it to be. Being alive is the meaning."
— Joseph Campbell, American mythologist

"Take on challenges and go after your goals without any regard for the people who tell you that you can't or try to stop you. That way, even if you fail you win, because if you fail on your terms you're a winner."

Paul Stanley, American musician

"*Happiness can be found, even in the darkest of times, if one only remembers to turn on the light.*"

JK Rowling, British writer

"There are two ways of spreading light — to be the candle or the mirror that reflects it."

Edith Wharton, American novelist

"The only person you are destined to become is the person you decide to be."

Ralph Waldo Emerson, American philosopher

> "What you do makes a difference, and you have to decide what kind of difference you want to make."
> Jane Goodall, English anthropologist

"Risk! Risk anything! Care no more for the opinions of others, for those voices. Do the hardest thing on earth for you. Act for yourself. Face the truth."

Katherine Mansfield, New Zealand author

"The greatest glory in living lies not in never falling, but in rising every time we fall."
Nelson Mandela, South African president and activist

"When we are no longer able to change a situation, we're challenged to change ourselves."
— Victor Frankl, Austrian psychiatrist

"The future belongs to those who believe in the beauty of their dreams."
Eleanor Roosevelt, American first lady

"Regret for the things we did can be tempered by time; it is regret for the things we did not do that is inconsolable."

Sydney Smith, 19th century English essayist

> "Only put off till tomorrow what you are willing to die having left undone."
> Pablo Picasso, Spanish painter

"To achieve the impossible, it is precisely the unthinkable that must be thought."
Tom Robbins, American author

"The most difficult thing is the decision to act, the rest is merely tenacity. The fears are paper tigers. You can do anything you decide to do."

Amelia Earhart, American aviation pioneer

"They say that time changes things, but you actually have to change them yourself."

Andy Warhol, American artist

> "You are more than a human being, you are a human becoming."
> Og Mandino, American author

"When one door closes another door opens, but we often look so long and so regretfully upon the closed door that we don't see the ones which open for us."

Alexander Graham Bell, Scottish-American inventor

"It is not the mountain we conquer but ourselves."
Sir Edmund Hillary, New Zealand mountaineer, first to climb Everest

"Mountains cannot be surmounted except by winding paths."
Goethe, German philosopher

"Happiness is a butterfly, which when pursued, is always just beyond your grasp, but which, if you will sit down quietly, may alight upon you."
— Nathaniel Hawthorne, American writer

"I have always had to work hard; anyone who works as hard could do what I do."

Johann Sebastian Bach, German composer

"There came a time when the risk to remain tight in a bud was more painful than the risk it took to blossom."

Anais Nin, French author

"A pessimist is one who makes difficulties of his opportunities, and an optimist is one who makes opportunities of his difficulties."

Harry Truman, 33rd American president

"Life is not measured by the number of breaths we take, but by the moments that take our breath away."

Proverb

"Be who you are and say what you feel, because those who mind don't matter and those who matter don't mind."

Dr Seuss, American writer and cartoonist

"You don't regret what you do, you regret what you don't do."
Greta Garbo, American actress

"You have to take risks. We will only understand the miracle of life fully when we allow the unexpected to happen."
— Paulo Coelho, Brazilian author

"*Great acts are made up of small deeds.*"
Lao Tzu, Ancient Chinese philosopher

"Many of life's failures are people who did not realise how close they were to success when they gave up."

Thomas Edison, American inventor

"Our greatest weakness lies in giving up. The most certain way to succeed is always to try just one more time."

Thomas Edison, American inventor

> "We don't see things as they are.
> We see them as we are."
>
> — The Talmud

"The follies which a man regrets most in his life are those which he didn't commit when he had the opportunity."

Helen Rowland, American writer

"If people knew how hard I worked to get my mastery, it wouldn't seem so wonderful at all."

Michelangelo, 16th century Italian painter and poet

"Everything in life is writable about if you have the outgoing guts to do it, and the imagination to improvise. The worst enemy to creativity is self-doubt."

Sylvia Plath, American poet and novelist

"To me the greatest pleasure of writing is not what it's about, but the music the words make."

Truman Capote, American writer

"Far better is it to dare mighty things, to win glorious triumphs — even though chequered by failure — than to rank with those poor spirits who neither enjoy much nor suffer much, because they live in a grey twilight that knows not victory nor defeat."

Theodore Roosevelt, 26th American president

"The more I want to get something done, the less I call it work."

Richard Bach, American writer

"Without new experiences, something inside of us sleeps. The sleeper must awaken."

Frank Herbert, American author

> "Poor is the man whose pleasures depend on the permission of another."
> — Madonna, American entertainer

"Write while the heat is in you. The writer who postpones the recording of his thoughts uses an iron which has cooled to burn a hole with. He cannot inflame the minds of his audience."

Henry David Thoreau, American writer

"The men who try to do something and fail are infinitely better than those who try to do nothing and succeed."

Lloyd Jones, New Zealand author

"Courage is the power to let go of the familiar."

Raymond Lindquist, American pastor

"To see a world in a grain of sand, and heaven in a wild flower; to hold infinity in the palm of your hand, and eternity in an hour... That is inspiration."

William Blake, English Romantic poet

"Moderation is the feebleness and sloth of the soul, whereas ambition is the warmth and activity of it."

Francois La Rochefoucauld, French writer

"To be yourself in a world that is constantly trying to make you something else is the greatest accomplishment."

Ralph Waldo Emerson, American philosopher

"I made the record that my life had me make. Each one is like a diary."

Lenny Kravitz, American entertainer

"I would much rather have regrets about not doing what people said, than regretting not doing what my heart led me to and wondering what life would have been like if I'd just been myself."

Brittany Renee, English author and dancer

> "Be like a postage stamp.
> Stick to one thing until you get there."
>
> Josh Billings, American writer

"Joy in the universe, and keen curiosity about it all. That has been my religion."

John Burroughs, American naturalist and author

"Breathe. Let go. And remind yourself that this very moment is the only one you know you have for sure."
Oprah Winfrey, American TV host

"There is no failure except in no longer trying."
Elbert Hubbard, American philosopher

"I'm a pilgrim of life, so from that point of view, I'm on a pilgrimage every day. Once one lives as a pilgrim, one lives lightly on the earth, with both detachment and engagement. It's all a pilgrimage."

Satish Kumar, Indian magazine editor

"Your regrets aren't what you did, but what you didn't do. So I take every opportunity."
Cameron Diaz, American actress

"Failure doesn't mean you are a failure, it just means you haven't succeeded yet."

Robert Schuller, American pastor and author

"*Criticism is something we can avoid easily — by saying nothing, doing nothing, and being nothing.*"

Aristotle, fourth century BCE Greek philosopher

"Language is the blood of the soul into which thoughts run and out of which they grow."

Oliver Wendell Holmes, American poet

"Anyone who has never made a mistake has never tried anything new."

Albert Einstein, German-Swiss physicist

*"Don't ask what the world needs.
Ask what makes you come alive, and go do it.
Because what the world needs is people who have come alive."*

Howard Thurman, American author and activist

> "We either make ourselves miserable, or we make ourselves strong. The amount of work is the same."
> — Carlos Castaneda, Peruvian-American author

"Just don't give up trying to do what you really want to do.
Where there is love and inspiration, I don't think you can go wrong."

Ella Fitzgerald, American jazz singer

"Always dream and shoot higher than you know how to. Don't bother just to be better than your contemporaries or predecessors. Try to be better than yourself."

William Faulkner, American author

"Supposing you have tried and failed again and again. You may have a fresh start any moment you choose, for this thing we call 'failure' is not the falling down, but the staying down."

Mary Pickford, Canadian actor and film pioneer

"Genius is one per cent inspiration and ninety-nine per cent perspiration."

Thomas Edison, American inventor

"*No one can make you feel inferior without your consent.*"
Eleanor Roosevelt, American first lady and activist

"We must be willing to let go of the life we have planned, so as to accept the life that is waiting for us."

Joseph Campbell, American mythologist

"The miracle is not to walk on water. The miracle is to walk on the green earth, dwelling deeply in the present moment and feeling truly alive."

Thich Nhat Hanh, Vietnamese monk

*"Rest not. Life is sweeping by;
go and dare before you die.
Something mighty and sublime,
leave behind to conquer time."*

— Goethe, German philosopher

"Let us be grateful to people who make us happy, they are the charming gardeners who make our souls blossom."

Marcel Proust, French author

"One's destination is never a place, but a new way of seeing things."
Henry Miller, American novelist

"Sometimes you've got to let everything go — purge yourself. If you're unhappy with anything, whatever is bringing you down, get rid of it. Because when you're free, your true creativity, your true self, comes out."

Tina Turner, American singer

"What lies behind us and what lies before us are tiny matters compared to what lies within us."

Ralph Waldo Emerson, American philosopher

"A child can teach an adult three things: to be happy for no reason, to always be busy with something, and to know how to demand with all his might that which he desires."

Paulo Coelho, Brazilian author

"Any technology, no matter how primitive, is magic to those who do not understand it."

Mark Stanley, comic creator

> "The major problems in the world are the result of the difference between how nature works and the way people think."
>
> Gregory Bateson, British anthropologist

"I don't believe in failure. It's not failure if you enjoyed the process."
Oprah Winfrey, American TV host

"Things turn out best for the people who make the best out of the way things turn out."

Art Linkletter, Canadian TV host

> "Dance like nobody's watching;
> love like you've never been hurt.
> Sing like nobody's listening;
> live like it's heaven on earth."
>
> — Irish proverb

"Life is really simple, but we insist on making it complicated."
Confucius, fifth century BCE Chinese philosopher

"A man of ordinary talent will always be ordinary, whether he travels or not; but a man of superior talent will go to pieces if he remains forever in the same place."
Wolfgang Amadeus Mozart, Austrian composer

"The man who goes alone can start today; but he who travels with another must wait till that other is ready."

Henry David Thoreau, American writer

"*I don't need anyone to rectify my existence. The most profound relationship we will ever have is the one with ourselves.*"

Shirley MacLaine, American actor and writer

"Life is a series of near misses. A lot of what we ascribe to luck is not luck at all, it's seizing the day and accepting responsibility for your future. It's seeing what other people don't see and pursuing that vision."

Howard Schultz, American businessman

"Imagination is the beginning of creation. You imagine what you desire, you will what you imagine then you create what you will."

George Bernard Shaw, Irish playwright

"Stop worrying about the potholes in the road and celebrate the journey."
Fitzhugh Mullan, American physician and writer

"Destiny is not a matter of chance, it is a matter of choice.
It is not a thing to be waited for, it is a thing to be achieved."

William Jennings Bryan, American politician and lawyer

"You cannot teach a man anything;
you can only help him find it within himself."
Galileo Galilei, Italian scientist

"In their freedom, birds make expanding circles in the sky. How do they learn to be free? They fall — and by falling are given wings to fly."

Rumi, 13th century Persian poet

"Do not fear death so much, but rather the inadequate life."
Bertolt Brecht, German poet and playwright

"You give but little when you give of your possessions.
It is when you give of yourself that you truly give."

Kahlil Gibran, Lebanese poet

"The distance is nothing; it is only the first step that is difficult."

Madame du Deffand, French hostess and patron of the arts

"Things may come to those who wait — but only the things left by those who hustle."

Abraham Lincoln, 16th American president

> "Not I – nor anyone else – can travel that road for you. You must travel it for yourself."
>
> Walt Whitman, American writer

"With the new day comes new strength and new thoughts."

Eleanor Roosevelt, American first lady

"We do not need magic to change the world, we carry all the power we need inside ourselves already — we have the power to imagine better."
JK Rowling, British writer

"Start by doing what's necessary; then do what's possible, and suddenly you are doing the impossible."
— Saint Francis of Assisi

"Cherish your visions and your dreams,
as they are the children of your soul,
the blueprints of your ultimate accomplishments."
Napoleon Hill, American writer

"Be glad of life, because it gives you the chance to love and to work and to play and to look up at the stars."
Henry Van Dyke, American writer

"Life is like music;
it must be composed by ear,
feeling and instinct, not by rule."

Samuel Butler, English novelist

"Sometimes good things fall apart so better things can come together."

Marilyn Monroe, American actress

"The aim of life is to live, and to live means to be aware — joyously, drunkenly, serenely, divinely aware."

Henry Miller, American novelist

"Everyone who got where he is had to begin where he was."
Richard L Evans, American writer

"There is no path to truth.
Truth must be discovered, but there is no formula for its discovery.
You must set out on the uncharted sea, and the uncharted sea is yourself."

Krishnamurti, Indian writer and philosopher

"No journey carries one far — unless, as it extends into the world around us, it goes an equal distance into the world within."

Lillian Smith, American writer

"One of the greatest discoveries a man makes, one of his greatest surprises, is to find that he can do what he was afraid he couldn't do."

Henry Ford, American businessman

www.ingramcontent.com/pod-product-compliance
Lightning Source LLC
Chambersburg PA
CBHW032039090426

42744CB00004B/62